From Baseball Mitts

To Oven Mitts
A Mothers of Sons Cookbook

Acknowledgements

I would like to thank the following people for their help, guidance, input and patience; for without them this project would never have come to fruition.

Jessica Manelis: my graphic designer- for her unending devotion and talent formatting and providing the graphics for the book.

Scott Frank: Personal Chef Graduate Magna Cum Laude Honors from Johnson & Wales University for consultation on the recipes and cooking techniques.

Barbara Mirsky: for her wit and ability creating the title of the book.

Rabbi Geri Newburge: for her invaluable editing and insight in the development of the book.

Lynny Ravitz: for her encouragement and long distance phone calls meant the world to me.

Robin Sue Landsburg: for her editing skills, cooking advice and recipes are always priceless.

Roberta Budman: for her love of my cooking inspired me and her typing skills (made my life so much easier).

Kay Goodstadt: for her expertise as a published author and media specialist helped me with the process of publishing and marketing this book.

Linda Skupp, Laura Salkin, Terry Blau, Carol Levin and Deb Berger: for generously submitting recipes to me.

Ed Wolfson, Amy Krell, and Lindsey Sullivan: for their editing skills, assuring me that typos would be at a minimum.

Sheila Stern: for sewing the apron and oven mitt.

Sheena Morales: for her help as my publicist.

My oldest son, *Justin:* for his love for my meatballs was the spark that ignited my continued journey to please the family with new recipes.

My second son, *Jared:* for his advice, knowledge and support helped me on a daily basis throughout this process.

My youngest son, *Seth:* for his desire to learn how to cook helped me come to the conclusion that this book would be useful.

My husband, *Howard:* for his confidence and expertise allowed me to "walk the walk".

Table of Contents

We created the Mothers of Sons community because...

Mom's with sons share a common bond. This bond is unique and gives us an instantaneous connection. We are a population that often needs more recognition. In many instances marketing efforts and commercial products are geared toward mothers with daughters. I have found it to be a struggle to buy presents for my sons. It is difficult, if not impossible, to find something that truly connects mother and son. Thus became my mission to fill that void. Consequently, my mission to fill that void was born. My objective was to create something that would be meaningful, useful and functional for my grown sons. I wanted something that would be timeless and could be handed down to future generations. A prerequisite was that the process had to be meaningful and enriching for me.

Cooking is one of my passions. I learned to cook out of necessity as a young woman, having married a man who had no interest or skill in the kitchen.

My mother and mother-in-law became my mentors, and I was quite the avid student. I availed myself of every opportunity to observe them in the kitchen. After mastering the fundamentals, I began to experiment with recipes and to develop my own. As I raised three sons, my skills were refined and my recipes multiplied. Anyone fortunate enough to be blessed with sons knows that food becomes a focal point in their daily lives. One meal seems to blend into the next with snacking interspersed. This book is the product of merging my passion for cooking with my desire to provide a useful, informative and meaningful connection.

This cookbook is dual-purposed and designed for young men between 18-35. If they are living in an off-campus apartment, single and working in the city or suburbs, or just fed up with expensive take-out. Many of these young men were too busy as they grew up or had no desire to learn the basics of cooking in the kitchen.

This book contains simple recipes with common ingredients (many of which should be contained in their pantries). It also helps with setting up the basic kitchen, includes tips and suggests the utensils needed for each dish.

How often can you find a great gift that brings both pleasure to you and your son and is useful as well? There is a little bit of MOM on every page!

Each recipe is named for a friend with sons. This circle of friends, family and coworkers helped with the challenges faced throughout this journey; as therapists, editors, cheerleaders, guinea pigs and critics. It is with love that I honor each one of them.

1

Food For Thought
When Using This Book

Before cooking, first review all the pages and familiarize yourself with the tips; they are useful in many of the recipes, even if they are not repeated, i.e. washing and piercing potatoes prior to cooking them in the microwave, or peeling onions before cooking.

Plan your menus. The list of ingredients in the beginning of each recipe make it easy for you to complete your shopping list. Organization, it will save time and make cooking more enjoyable.

At the bottom of each page are illustrations suggesting the utensils you need for that recipe. Before you start cooking, have them readily available.

These recipes are mainly guidelines. With the exception of baking, cooking is not an exact science (often differing brands package items in varying amounts). One brand of pasta sauce may be 24 ounces, whereas another may be 20 ounces. If you can't find the exact measurements in the recipe, just experiment. Chances are you may like your version even better than mine!

Have fun and practice. You can adjust seasonings and vary certain ingredients.

Just taste, taste, taste and invite your mom over when you have perfected the dish. Chances are, no matter what, she'll tell you that it was fabulous!

When in doubt, call your mother!!!

Setting Up Your Kitchen

Setting up your kitchen is an exciting endeavor. You'll be surprised how little time you will spend cooking, when you have the proper utensils and equipment. With an organized kitchen, cooking will become that much more enjoyable.

Now you can appreciate all the years your mom shopped, prepared and cooked meals for you!

Utensils:

Knives: Always buy the best you can afford as these will be used most often. You need the following basic sizes:
- large cutting (8" blade also called Chef or French knife)
- small cutting (also called a paring knife)
- bread knife (serrated blade)
- set of steak knives

Measuring cups: there are 2 kinds dry and liquid; both come in sets.

Measuring spoons: come in a set of assorted sizes.

Spatulas: come in many shapes and sizes. Make sure you have at least a silicone one that is large enough to flip a medium sized pancake.

Basting brush: a silicone one can be tossed in the dishwasher after using.

Ladle: a deep one is useful.

Potato peeler: straight peelers (which are easier to use) or y-peelers (the blade is perpendicular to the handle).

Bottle opener: a hand held one is the easiest and cheapest to have.

Can opener: these are available in electric or manual models.

Ice cream scoop: a stainless steel one with or without a spring loaded lever.

Set of wooden spoons: at least 3 in varied sizes.

Pizza cutter: comes in varied sizes and materials. Look for one that's easy to clean.

Corkscrew: a winged corkscrew is inexpensive and easy to use.

Kitchen tongs: come in 9, 12 and 16 inch lengths. The 12 inch are the best. You should look for ones that have scalloped slightly cupped as these most easily grip food.

Equipment:

Cookware: (buy the best you can afford; heavy aluminum or stainless steel last a long time)
- Sauce pans- 3, 4 quart with lids and 2 larger Dutch Oven pots with covers (at least 6 3/4 quart and 8 quart)
- 10"-12" fry pan-non-stick is a good choice
- 12" non stick grill pan
- 12" sauté/ fry pan-this pan is deeper and comes with a cover

Assorted sizes of microwaveable baking dishes: (glass is good for oven or microwave) including the following sizes:

- 8" x 8"
- 9" x 12"-18"
- 13" x 9"

Mixing Bowls: usually come in a set of 3 (glass or ceramic can be used in the microwave for heating things) which usually nest , saves space.

Cutting Boards: (plastic can be washed in the dishwasher). Try to select ones that are at least 12" x 18" and 3/4" thick to avoid warping. You should have 2; one for vegetables and fruit the other for meat and chicken.

Toaster ovens: come in varying sizes and also can double as convection ovens/broilers too.

Colander: a metal one can double as a steamer (just partially fill a pot with water, bring it to a simmer and place the colander on top- a do-it yourself steamer!) If space is limited the collapsible ones are a good choice.

Spoon rest: a small dish or saucer will serve as one as well.

Cookie sheets: come with or without rims. Rimmed ones can double as cooking pans. Buy heavy weight aluminum that will last as you will use these often.

Graters: there are 2 kinds- box and microplane graters. If your budget only allows you to purchase one, I suggest the microplane. Many products can be purchased already grated.

Trash can: a fairly large one so you don't have to keep running out with the trash.

Oven mitts and potholders: (at least 2) either washable or silicone.

Tea kettles: come in varying materials with or without whistle. One with a removable top is easier to clean.

Coffee maker: priced for any budget and many different sizes.

Electric hand mixer: can be purchased inexpensively.

Hand-held immersion blender: also called a stick blender, it can be used to puree soups or other foods right in the container.

Meat thermometer: digital ones are easy to read.

Dish towels: always have at least 3 on hand.

Notes:

Setting Up Your Pantry

As Julia Child, one of the greatest cooks, said: "You don't have to cook fancy or complicated masterpieces – just good food from fresh ingredients".

Of course, everyone has individual tastes when it comes to seasonings, and I encourage you to always experiment. You would be surprised how a little bit of basil, garlic or other spices, totally changes the flavors of a dish.

Setting up your pantry is the second most important step in your journey from **Baseball Mitts to Oven Mitts**. The following is a list of ingredients that are considered staples and should be part of everyone's basic pantry.

For Baking:
All purpose pre-sifted flour
Baking powder
Baking soda
Chocolate chips
Chopped almonds
Chopped pecans
Chopped walnuts
Cornstarch
Cream of tartar
Golden raisins
Regular raisins
White and brown sugar

Spices:
Black pepper
Cinnamon
Dried and fresh basil
Dry mustard
Garlic powder
Ginger powder
Hungarian paprika
Italian seasoning
Jar of minced or fresh garlic (needs to be refrigerated)
Jar of minced ginger (needs to be refrigerated)
Nutmeg
Onion powder
Oregano
Salt
Vanilla

Condiments:
Balsamic vinegar
Barbecue Sauce
Canola cooking spray
Canola or vegetable oil
Extra virgin olive oil
Honey
Hot sauce
Ketchup
Mayonnaise
Mustard
Soy sauce
White vinegar
Worcestershire sauce

Miscellaneous:
Jelly
Lemons or lemon juice
Marinara sauce or pasta sauce
Pasta
Peanut butter
Rice
Selection of cheese including cheddar and mozzarella
Tomato paste
Whole canned tomatoes

Notes:

snacks

cocktails

munchies

appetizers

TIDBITS

dips

11

Janis K's Kan't Get Enough Cheese And Potato Soup

1 large baking potato
1 can cheddar cheese soup (10 ounces)
1 1/2 cups chicken stock

1.   Microwave the potato wrapped in a paper towel for 8 minutes on High.
2. Carefully remove it from the microwave using oven mitts. It will be HOT! Set aside until cool enough to touch.
3. When the potato is cool, cut it into 1/2 inch cubes.
4. Add the cheese soup and chicken stock to a medium saucepan.
5. Bring it to a simmer, stirring occasionally over medium high heat.
6. Add the potato and continue to heat soup for 5 minutes.

TIP

Never store potatoes in plastic bags. Storing them in paper helps keep moisture out so they won't spoil.

TIP

Ladle soup into bowls and garnish with a dollop of sour cream and a few chopped scallions if desired.

Microwave

Paper towels

Medium saucepan

Joyce H's Serve It Hot Beef And Mushroom Soup

2 tablespoons butter or margarine
1 package sliced fresh mushrooms (8 ounces)
1 small yellow onion sliced in 1/8 inch slices
1 can beef broth (14 ounces)
1 1/4 cups water
1 envelope onion-mushroom soup mix

1. In a medium saucepan melt the margarine or butter over medium high heat.
2. Add the mushrooms and sliced onion and cook until tender, for about 5 minutes.
3. Stir in the water, beef broth and soup mix.
4. Continue cooking on medium heat until it starts to boil.
5. Reduce to low heat and cook for an additional 5 minutes.

TIP

Do not wash mushrooms until you are ready to use them to prevent spoilage.

TIP

Mushrooms should be removed from the plastic container when brought home from the market and stored in an open paper bag with a folded paper towel so they do not get moist.

Medium saucepan

Phyllis R's Outstanding Onion Soup With Steak

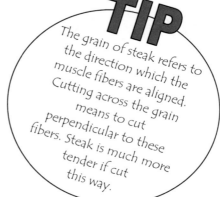

1 tablespoon olive oil
1 piece of flank steak, about 4 ounces
1 large yellow onion sliced in 1/4 inch rounds
1 teaspoon sugar
1 tablespoon fresh minced garlic
1 tablespoon balsamic vinegar
2 cups beef stock
italian or french bread, optional

TIP
The grain of steak refers to the direction which the muscle fibers are aligned. Cutting across the grain means to cut perpendicular to these fibers. Steak is much more tender if cut this way.

1. Heat 1/2 tablespoon of oil in a large pan with a cover over medium heat.
2. Add the steak and cook 2 to 3 minutes per side, or to your preference.
3. Transfer the steak to a cutting board and let it stand for 5 minutes.
4. Add the remaining oil to the pan and heat it over medium low heat.
5. Cook the onion along with the sugar in the pan, stirring occasionally for about 20 minutes or until the onions are golden brown.
6. Add the garlic and cook a few minutes more.
7. Increase the heat to medium high, add the vinegar and bring it to a boil.
8. Cook stirring until the vinegar is almost evaporated.
9. Add the beef stock and bring it to another boil.
10. Let the soup simmer over medium low heat, cover, and cook for 15 minutes more.
11. Divide the soup evenly into 2 bowls (you may add a slice of french or italian bread if desired.)
12. Slice steak across the grain into thin strips and add it to soup bowls.

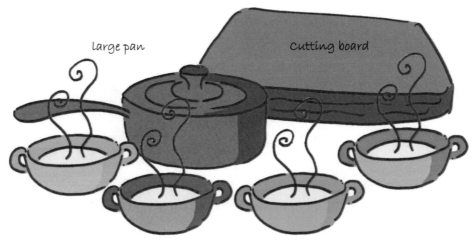

large pan

cutting board

Adi G's Awesome Apple And Squash Soup

1 package diced butternut squash (found in the produce section)
3 tablespoons butter or margarine
3 small apples cored, peeled and cut in 1/2 inch slices (see tip)
1 medium yellow onion chopped in 1/2 inch pieces
1 box vegetable broth (32 ounces)
1/4 teaspoon nutmeg
heavy cream (optional)

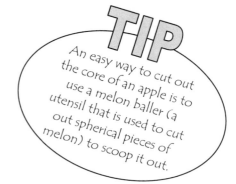

TIP
An easy way to cut out the core of an apple is to use a melon baller (a utensil that is used to cut out spherical pieces of melon) to scoop it out.

1. Melt the butter in a large saucepan over medium heat.
2. Add the onions and continue cooking them in the saucepan over medium heat until brown.
3. Add the diced squash and vegetable broth.
4. Simmer on low heat until the squash is soft when pierced with a fork.
5. Add the apples and nutmeg and continue cooking on low heat until the apples are soft.
6. Let the soup cool then puree it (mash to a pudding like consistency) with a hand-held immersion blender or put it in a regular blender.
7. When serving swirl in a dash of cream if desired.

TIP
The best kind of apples for cooking are gala, red or golden delicious, empire, courtland, honeycrisp, rome or pink lady.

Blender

Large saucepan

Toby W's Serve It All Day Scallion Dip

1 cup mayonnaise
1 cup sour cream
1/2 cup sliced scallions (white and green parts)
1 teaspoon dijon mustard
1/2 teaspoon fresh minced garlic

TIP
If you want to cut the calories, use light sour cream and mayonnaise.

1. In a blender mix all the ingredients until smooth.
2. Place in a small bowl, cover with plastic wrap and chill.

TIP
To cut the scallions, wash well, remove the thin skin, cut off the ends and slice on the outside; into small pieces.

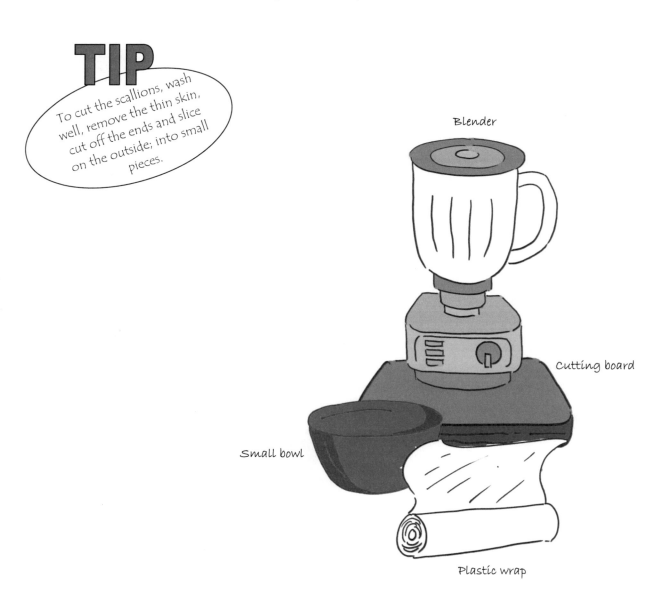

Blender

Cutting board

Small bowl

Plastic wrap

Lori S's Summer Spinach Bread Dip

1 envelope vegetable soup mix
2 cups sour cream
1 box frozen spinach (10 ounces)
1 loaf large round bread

TIP
You can serve this along with cut carrots, celery, broccoli, peppers or other fresh vegetables.

1. Thaw the frozen spinach in the refrigerator before cooking it (thawed spinach cooks more evenly than frozen).
2. Fill a medium saucepan that has a lid with water and heat it to a boil over medium high heat.
3. Put the thawed spinach in the saucepan, cover it and continue cooking it to another full boil over the medium high heat.
4. Lower the heat to medium low and cook for 3-5 minutes.
5. Remove the spinach from the pan, drain in a colander and let the spinach cool. Squeeze out any excess water.
6. Pour off the excess water from sour cream if there is any.
7. Mix sour cream, cooled spinach and soup mix in a large bowl.
8. Cover with plastic wrap and chill for at least 2 hours.
9. Slice a circle around the top of the bread and set it aside. Remove the inside part of the bread by scooping it out and cut it into 2 inch pieces (make sure you don't cut through the bread).
10. Fill the hole of the bread with dip. You can use the circle that you cut out above to cover the bread until you serve it.

TIP
Using a serrated knife makes cutting the bread easier.

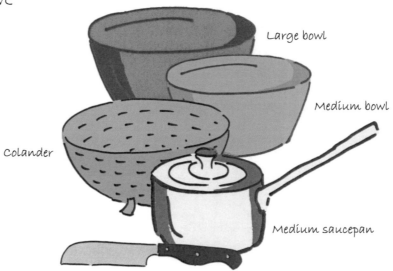

Large bowl

Medium bowl

Colander

Medium saucepan

Sharp serrated knife

Melanie G's Got To Have It Dip

1 container of sour cream (16 ounces)
1 envelope onion soup mix
1/4 cup cheddar cheese

1. In a medium bowl combine all the ingredients.
2. Cover with plastic wrap and chill for at least 4 hours.

TIP
Serve with chips or cut vegetables.

TIP
To make an easy and pretty centerpiece fill a glass vase with whole lemons, limes or apples.

TIP
You can add bacon, chopped scallions, garlic powder or other spices to create varieties of this dip.

TIP
A nice way to serve this dip for a party, is to scoop out the seeds from a green or red pepper and fill it with the dip.

Plastic wrap

Medium bowl

Bev F's Buffalo Cream Cheese Dip

TIP
You can add 1/2 cup shredded cheddar cheese and 1/2 cup of ranch dressing to change it up.

2 large boneless, skinless chicken breast halves
6 tablespoons hot sauce (to make dip mildly hot)
1 package cream cheese, cut into 1-inch chunks (8 ounces)

Preheat oven to 350°

1. Place the chicken breasts in a medium size saucepan filled with water.
2. Bring it to a boil over high heat.
3. Reduce heat to medium, cover and cook until done for approximately 7 minutes.
4. Remove the chicken from the water and allow it to cool.
5. Shred the chicken using 2 forks (see tip).
6. Put the shredded chicken in a small baking pan, mix in the cream cheese and hot sauce, (add more hot sauce to make this spicier).
7. Warm it in the oven until all the cheese is melted.

TIP
To shred the chicken using forks, insert the fork, with back sides facing each other, into the center of the meat. Gently pull them away from each other, shredding the chicken.

TIP
Spread leftover dip (if there is any) on a roll and have for lunch the next day.

Medium saucepan

Small baking pan

Cathy O's Nighttime Nachos

tortilla chips
3/4 cup shredded monterey cheese
1/4 cup shredded cheddar cheese
canola cooking spray

Preheat oven to 350°

1. Line a rimmed cookie sheet with aluminum foil and spray it with cooking spray.
2. Spread out the tortilla chips overlapping some.
3. Sprinkle the chips with both cheeses.
4. Bake for about 5 minutes or until cheese is melted.

TIP

If you have a ceramic serving plate that is oven-proof, you can bake the nachos directly on it. This saves clean up time!

TIP

You can add cut up cooked chicken, salsa, green pepper or onion for a variation.

TIP

Heat this in the microwave in a microwaveable pan if you don't want to heat up the kitchen.

Cookie sheet

Canola cooking spray

Randi G's Grilled Bread With Ricotta And Zucchini

4 1/2 inch thick slices country bread
2 tablespoons olive oil
2 zucchini thinly sliced lengthwise
1 cup fresh basil, leaves torn (found in the produce department)
kosher salt
1 cup fresh ricotta

TIP You can make this on outdoor grill or inside using a grill pan.

1. Heat the grill to medium high heat.
2. Brush the bread with 1 tablespoon oil and grill until golden and crisp, about 1 minute per side.
3. Transfer to plates.
4. Grill the zucchini until tender and slightly charred, 3-4 minutes per side.
5. Toss in a large bowl with the basil, 1/2 tsp salt, and the remaining oil.
6. Top the bread with the zucchini slices then add a spoonful of ricotta cheese.

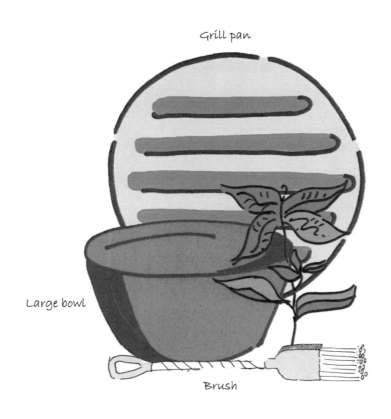

Grill pan

Large bowl

Brush

Ruthie C's Great Garlic Knots

1 pound pizza dough, thawed if frozen
4 tablespoons olive oil
2 teaspoons fresh minced garlic
salt and black pepper
all purpose flour for shaping dough

Preheat oven to 400°

TIP

To Freeze: Prepare through step 7, using a baking sheet lined with parchment paper; freeze until firm, for 1 hour. Transfer to a resealable plastic bag, freeze up to 3 months.

1. Cover a large rimmed cookie sheet with parchment paper.
2. Mix the minced garlic and olive oil together in a small bowl.
3. On a lightly floured work surface (table or counter), roll out dough to a rectangle about 16 by 10 inches.
4. With a knife or pizza cutter, cut the dough horizontally into 16 strips 1 by 10 inches
5. Take a strip of dough, carefully tie into a knot, dip it into the olive oil and garlic mixture and place it on the cookie sheet that is covered with parchment paper.
1. Repeat 15 more times.
2. Lightly sprinkle with salt and black pepper.
3. Bake for 8-10 minutes or until golden brown.

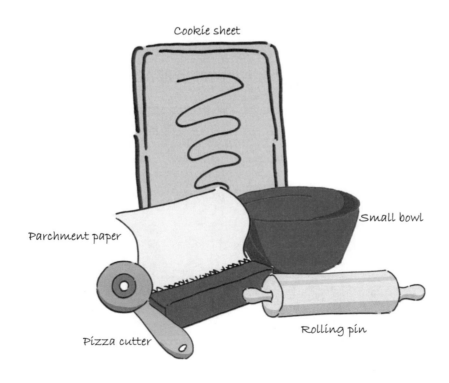

Cookie sheet

Small bowl

Parchment paper

Rolling pin

Pizza cutter

Elise M's Munchie Party Cheese Thins

1 cup instant potato flakes
3 tablespoons sharp cheese spread
2 tablespoons margarine or butter
2 tablespoons all purpose flour
1/2 teaspoon salt
1/4 teaspoon hungarian paprika
1 tablespoon cold water

Preheat oven to 425°

TIP
To knead the dough, place the dough on a floured surface and use the heel of your hand (fleshy part of the palm) to compress and push dough away from you. Keep turning it and repeating this incorporates all the ingredients uniformly.

1. Mix all the ingredients in a medium bowl to make a dough (make sure the water you use is cold).
2. Knead the dough with your hands for 2 minutes (see tip).
3. Shape the dough using your hands, into a long roll about 10 inches long and 1 inch around.
4. Wrap it completely in plastic wrap and refrigerate the wrapped dough for at least 2 hours.
5. Remove the plastic, and slice it into 1/2 inch slices and place the slices about 1 inch apart on an ungreased cookie sheet.
6. Bake for about 10 minutes or until lightly browned.

TIP
When you can't find the end of the plastic wrap, rub a little flour around the roll. It helps to find the beginning.

TIP
Make sure your hands and the surface are lightly floured when you need the dough.

Cookie sheet

Medium bowl

Plastic wrap

Carol M's Mangia Onion Cheese Bread

1 medium yellow onion chopped in 1/2 inch pieces
3 tablespoons margarine or butter
1 1/2 cups buttermilk baking mix
1 1/2 cups milk
1 egg, beaten
1 cup shredded cheddar cheese
canola cooking spray

TIP

Olive oil should be stored in a dark-tinted glass bottle or tin since exposure to light and heat destroys the oil's flavor. Always keep your oil in a cabinet away from the stove. The shelf life of olive oil is two years.

Preheat oven to 400°

1. Grease a 8 X 8 square baking pan with butter or cooking spray.
2. Mix the onion and 1 tablespoon of butter or margarine in a small microwaveable bowl.
3. Microwave the onion on high about 2 minutes until tender.
4. Mix the buttermilk baking mix, milk and egg until moistened in a separate medium bowl.
5. Stir in the onion mixture and 1/2 cup of the cheddar cheese.
6. Spread the mixture in the prepared pan and top it with 2 tablespoons of margarine.
7. Sprinkle with the remaining 1/2 cup of cheese.
8. Bake for about 20 minutes or until a toothpick from the center comes out clean.

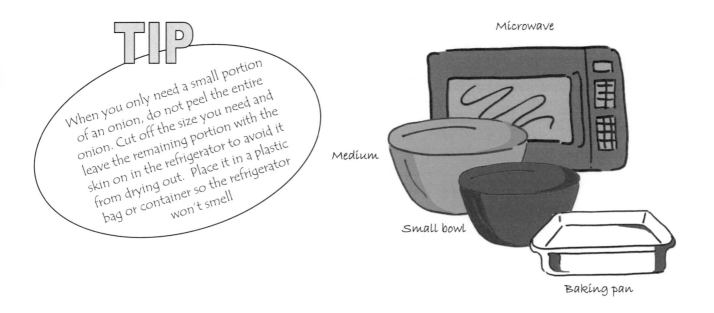

TIP

When you only need a small portion of an onion, do not peel the entire onion. Cut off the size you need and leave the remaining portion with the skin on in the refrigerator to avoid it from drying out. Place it in a plastic bag or container so the refrigerator won't smell

Microwave

Medium

Small bowl

Baking pan

Robin Sue L's Roll Ups

1 large loaf of white bread
3/4 cup grated cheddar cheese
1/2 cup margarine at room temperature
1/8 teaspoon garlic powder
grated zucchini and/or chopped mushrooms (optional)
canola cooking spray

TIP
To clean a wooden rolling pin never soak it in water. Just use a damp sponge or brush it off with a dry cloth.

Preheat oven to 400°

1. Mix together the grated cheese, margarine and garlic powder in a medium bowl and set aside (if desired you may add the grated zucchini and/or chopped mushrooms).
2. Take 5 slices of bread at a time and cut off the crusts.
3. Using a rolling pin, roll each slice of trimmed bread until flattened on a cutting board or a piece of waxed paper on the counter.
4. Spread each piece of flattened bread with the cheese mixture.
5. Roll from point to point side down and place on a rimmed cookie sheet.
6. Repeat steps #3 to #5 until all the bread is used.
7. Place all the unbaked roll ups in the freezer until you are ready to serve.
8. When ready to serve, spray a rimmed cookie sheet with canola cooking spray and place frozen rollups in a single layer.
9. Bake for 10-15 minutes until golden brown.

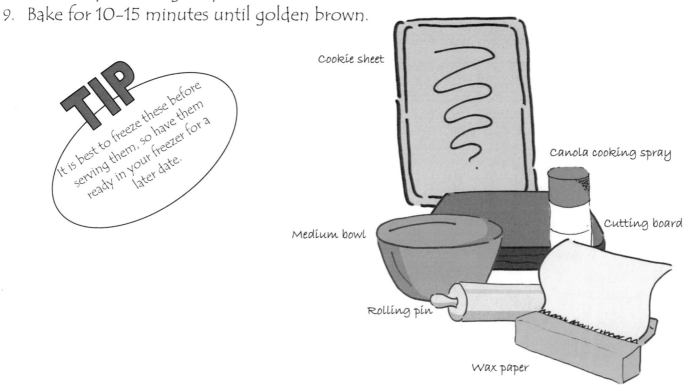

TIP
It is best to freeze these before serving them, so have them ready in your freezer for a later date.

Cookie sheet

Canola cooking spray

Cutting board

Medium bowl

Rolling pin

Wax paper

Reatha B's Mini Cream Cheese Roll Ups

1 package cream cheese (8 ounces)
1 loaf sliced white bread (cut off crusts)
1 lightly beaten egg yolk
1/4 cup sugar
1/2 cup melted butter or margarine
cinnamon
sugar

TIP

Having a carton of egg whites on hand is a good thing.

Preheat oven to 400°

1. Beat together cream cheese, egg yolk and sugar in a large mixing bowl.
2. Using a rolling pin, roll each slice of trimmed bread until flattened on a cutting board or a piece of waxed paper on the counter.
3. Spread each piece of flattened bread with the cream cheese mixture.
4. Roll from point to point side down and place on a rimmed cookie sheet.
5. Dip each roll up log in the melted butter.
6. Sprinkle the roll ups lightly with cinnamon and sugar.
7. Wrap each roll in plastic wrap and freeze for at least a few hours.
8. When ready to serve, remove the logs from the freezer and cut each piece in half.
9. Place on an ungreased cookie sheet and bake for 10-13 minutes until golden brown.

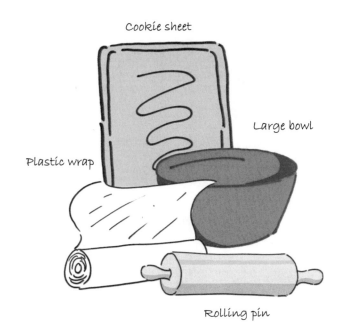

Cookie sheet

Large bowl

Plastic wrap

Rolling pin

TIP

To separate eggs: gently tap the egg against the rim of the bowl breaking it in half, attempting to break the egg evenly. Hold the egg so the crack is facing up. Pry open the egg in half so the yolk remains in the shell (do this over a bowl). Gently allow the white of the egg to slide into the bowl as you shift the yolk from one half of the shell to the other back and forth.

Shelly N's Best Buttermilk Batter Squares

1 1/2 cups buttermilk baking mix (found in the baking aisle)
1 egg, beaten
1 cup milk
1 large yellow onion
1 stick butter or margarine
1 cup grated cheddar cheese
canola cooking spray

TIP
A brand name for buttermilk biscuit mix is Bisquick.

Preheat oven to 400°

1. Spray a 9 x 13 baking pan with cooking spray.
2. Dice the onion into 1 inch squares and set aside.
3. Beat the egg and mix with milk in a medium mixing bowl. Add buttermilk biscuit mix to the bowl to make batter.
4. Melt 1/2 stick of margarine in a small skillet and sauté onion till brown.
5. Add the onion to the batter and 1/2 of grated cheese.
6. Pour the batter into prepared pan and sprinkle remaining cheese on top.
7. Put the other 1/2 stick of margarine in a small bowl and melt it in the microwave. After it's melted drizzle it on top of the mix.
8. Bake for 20-25 minutes, or until a toothpick comes out clean. Cool for 10 minutes and cut into squares.

TIP
Spray the bottom and sides of the baking pan well to avoid sticking.

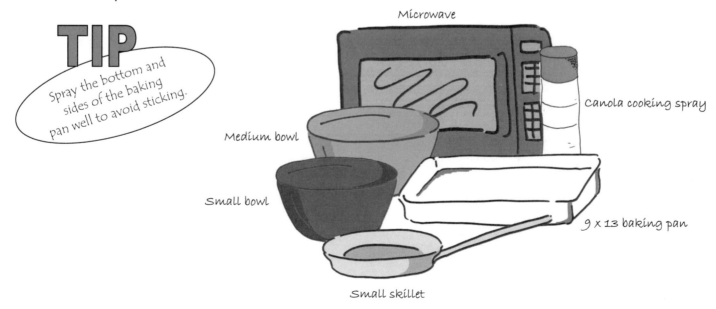

Microwave

Canola cooking spray

Medium bowl

Small bowl

9 x 13 baking pan

Small skillet

Beverly B's Boy Do I Like It Bruschetta

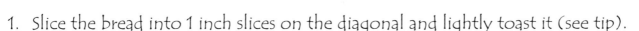

3 medium ripe tomatoes cut into 1/4 inch pieces
2 tablespoons chopped fresh basil leaves
2 teaspoons extra virgin olive oil
salt and black pepper
1/2 teaspoon garlic powder
1 loaf french bread

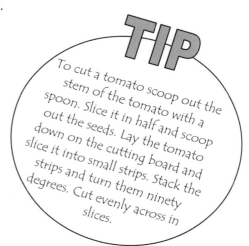

TIP

If you don't have a toaster oven, you can toast the bread on a cookie sheet at 350° for a few minutes.

1. Slice the bread into 1 inch slices on the diagonal and lightly toast it (see tip).
2. In a small bowl mix the tomatoes, chopped basil leaves, olive oil and garlic powder.
3. Add a small amount of salt and pepper. Taste it and add more if necessary.
4. Spoon the mixture onto bread and serve to your friends.

TIP

To cut a tomato scoop out the stem of the tomato with a spoon. Slice it in half and scoop out the seeds. Lay the tomato down on the cutting board and slice it into small strips. Stack the strips and turn them ninety degrees. Cut evenly across in slices.

Toaster Oven

Small bowl

Cutting Board

Rose H's Half Sour Pickles

6 – 13 kirby cucumbers
1 generous teaspoonful of commercial pickling spices
6-8 whole garlic cloves
1/8 teaspoon dill weed (optional)
4-6 dried red chili peppers (optional)
1/2 cup white vinegar
salt
water

1. Take a clean jar, from a quart size to a gallon size.
2. Wash 6 to 13 small kirby cucumbers, depending on the size of the jar.
3. Pour the commercial pickling spices into the jar.
4. Add 6 to 8 garlic cloves, unpeeled, which you've sliced in a few places, without cutting all the way through the clove.
5. Pack the cucumbers into the jar whole. Add the dill weed and chili peppers if you choose.
6. Add 3 to 4 ounces of white vinegar.
7. Fill a measuring cup with tap water hot enough to dissolve salt. To each cup of water add 1 teaspoon of salt and stir to thoroughly dissolve.
8. Pour the water into the jar, cupful by cupful, until the jar is full.
9. Cover and leave on the kitchen counter for two days.
10. Keep refrigerated until ready to eat.

Pickle jar

Cutting board

Measuring cup

TIP

Make your own pickling spices with the following ingredients: 2 tablespoons mustard seed, 1 tablespoon whole allspice, 2 teaspoons coriander seeds, 2 whole cloves garlic, 1 teaspoon ground ginger, 1 teaspoon dried red pepper flakes and 1 bay leaf, crumbled. Combine and store in an airtight container.

Bobby C's Shout Out Skewered Mozzarella Balls

10 mozzarella cheese balls
10 cherry or grape tomatoes
20 washed fresh basil leaves
extra virgin olive oil
balsamic vinegar
mixed greens
skewers

TIP
Mixed greens can be found in produce aisle of supermarket bagged or loose ready to use.

1. Cut the mozzarella balls in half.
2. Put on skewers in the following order: 1 tomato, 1 mozzarella ball, 1 folded basil leaf.
3. Repeat on the same skewer.
4. Continue making skewers until there are 5 completed.
5. Lay out the greens on a serving plate.
6. Place the finished skewers on the greens.
7. Drizzle the skewers with olive oil and balsamic vinegar.

TIP
No Skewers? Make smaller versions on a toothpick.

TIP
A great easy appetizer to impress your significant other, boss or your parents!

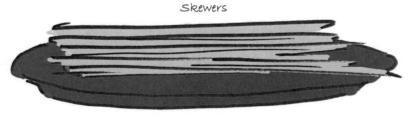

Skewers

Serving Platter

Gail S's Stuffed Goat Cheese Tomatoes

5 ripe tomatoes cut in half lengthwise
1/8 cup basil pesto (found in the italian section)
1/8 cup goat cheese
1 tablespoon fresh basil leafs snipped in small pieces
salt and black pepper
1/2 teaspoon olive oil

TIP
Dental Floss can be used to cut goat cheese. Just hold it perpendicular to the log of cheese and saw it back and forth to cut even slices.

Preheat oven to 400°

1. Pour the olive oil on a paper towel. Rub the towel on bottom of a medium baking pan to grease the bottom.
2. Lightly sprinkle the cut tomatoes with salt and black pepper.
3. Place the tomatoes cut side up in the pan.
4. Bake uncovered about 5 minutes or until the tomatoes are soft.
5. Divide the pesto and goat cheese evenly onto each tomato half.
6. Bake about 2 more minutes or until the cheese is soft.
7. Sprinkle with the cut basil before serving.

TIP
Try growing your own tomatoes in a container. It can be fun and easy.

Paper towels

Medium baking pan

Ferne W's Skewered Shrimp

12 large cooked, shelled and deveined shrimp
12 grape tomatoes
12 washed fresh basil leaves
12 skewers
1/2 cup balsamic vinaigrette dressing

1. Hold the shrimp like a letter C with the tail on the bottom.
2. Push the skewer through the tail, stopping when it hits the middle.
3. Skewer 1 grape tomato and 1 basil leaf.
4. Push the skewer through the rest of the shrimp.
5. Repeat until you have 12 skewers.
6. Drizzle the skewers with balsamic dressing and serve.

TIP
Chinese black vinegar can be used instead of balsamic vinegar.

TIP
When cutting basil leaves, use a kitchen scissor rather than a knife to prevent them from shredding.

TIP
Serve this as an appetizer or a main course on a hot summer night with a green salad.

Skewers

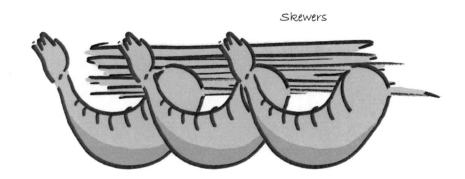

Deb B's Bites Of Marinated Salmon

1 pound of fresh salmon filet cut into 1 inch pieces
1/4 cup honey teriyaki dressing
1/4 cup light honey mustard dressing

Preheat oven to 500°

1. Mix the honey teriyaki dressing and the light honey mustard dressing in a plastic bag. Set aside.
2. Add the salmon pieces to the bag. Make sure the dressing mixes with all the salmon pieces.
3. Seal the bag and marinate in fridge overnight.
4. When ready to cook, drain dressing from the bag and discard bag and leftover dressing. Place the salmon pieces on a rimmed cookie sheet.
5. Cook for 3-4 minutes. Do not overcook!

TIP
Kitchen shears work well for cutting the salmon.

TIP
You can omit cutting the salmon into pieces and marinate the salmon filet whole. Bake at 500° for 10 minutes per inch of thickness.

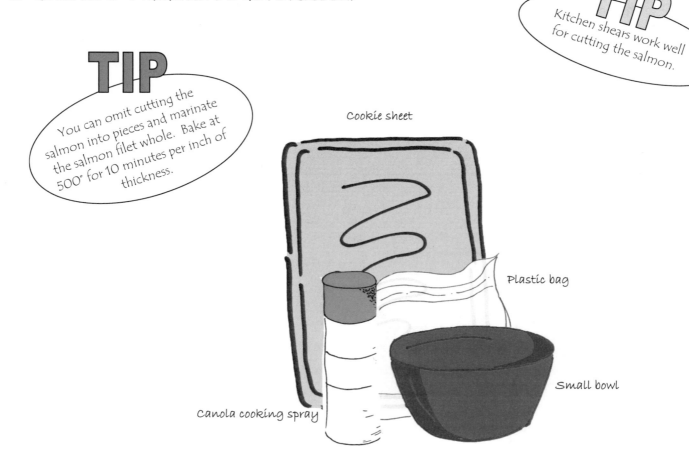

Cookie sheet

Plastic bag

Small bowl

Canola cooking spray

Francine N's Perfect Party Cheese Fondue

1 clove of fresh garlic cut in 1/2
2 cups shredded swiss cheese
2 cups shredded gruyere cheese
1/4 cup all purpose flour
1/4 teaspoon salt
1/4 teaspoon ground nutmeg powder
1 1/2 cups white wine
french bread, apples, celery, carrots for dipping

TIP
To remove the paper from a garlic clove, heat it in the microwave at 100% power for about 10 seconds. This creates steam that helps remove the skin.

1. Rub the inside of a large microwaveable dish with the garlic and then discard the garlic clove.
2. Combine the cheese, flour, salt and nutmeg in a large bowl.
3. Pour the wine into the casserole that was prepared with the garlic and microwave on medium for about 4 minutes (wine should be hot but not boiling).
4. Add the other ingredients to the dish and mix well.
5. Microwave on Medium until the cheese is bubbly for about 5-9 minutes.
6. Stir and serve.
7. Dip bread, apples, celery and carrots and enjoy.

Large bowl

Microwave dish

Rena A's Muffin Tin Mini Lasagnas

1/2 jar pasta sauce
1 package round wonton wrappers (found in the produce section)
1/2 pound grated mozzarella cheese
1/4 pound grated parmesan cheese
ricotta cheese (4 ounces)
olive oil cooking spray

TIP
Use the pasta sauce sparingly, if you use too much sauce the lasagnas will not hold their shape.

Preheat oven to 350°

1. Spray a muffin tin with olive oil cooking spray.
2. Line each well of the tin with 2 round wonton wrappers.
3. Layer the molds as follows: sprinkle parmesan cheese ,a spoonful of mozzarella, a spoonful of ricotta and a spoonful of sauce.
4. Repeat the above layering starting with wonton wrappers 4 more times ending with pasta sauce (or until the muffin wells are filled).
5. Bake until brown for about 20 min.

TIP
Sautéed vegetables can be added for a nice variety.

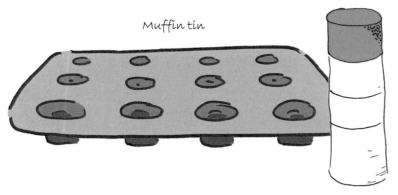

Muffin tin

Olive Oil cooking spray

Marcey P's Mini Burgers

1/2 teaspoon fresh minced garlic
1/4 cup mayonnaise
1/8 teaspoon lemon juice
1 pound of lean ground beef
1 small yellow onion chopped in 1/4 inch pieces
1 package of dinner rolls
salt

TIP
Serve with tomatoes, cheese, pickles or lettuce.

Heat oven to 350°

1. Place the minced garlic in a small bowl and sprinkle a dash of salt on top. Set the bowl aside.
2. In a large bowl, mix the ground beef with the onion. Form it into small patties and place them on a rimmed cookie sheet.
3. Cook for 9-11 minutes, flipping them halfway through cooking time (use a spatula for easy flipping).
4. While the burgers are cooking, add the mayonnaise to the garlic mixture from step 1 to form a paste.
5. Spread small dinner rolls with the garlic mayonnaise paste and assemble the finished burgers.

TIP
For a quick russian dressing mix ketchup, mayonnaise and relish for a great burger sauce.

Cookie sheet

Large bowl

Spatula

Small bowl

Amy K's Like Them Hot Chicken Wings

12 chicken wings
1 tablespoon garlic powder
2 teaspoons onion powder
4 tablespoons canola oil
2 tablespoons ketchup
1 tablespoon honey
4 teaspoons hot sauce
2 teaspoons chili powder (optional)

TIP

Keep honey in an airtight jar at room temperature. If it crystallizes and gets hard, put the jar in warm water (not boiling) until the crystals dissolve. This will get it back to liquid form.

Preheat oven to 425°

1. Line a rimmed cookie sheet or shallow pan with foil.
2. Cut off the tips of the wings (see tip).
3. Mix all the other ingredients in a small bowl to make the sauce.
4. Arrange the wings on the cookie sheet or pan in a single layer.
5. Pour the sauce over the wings.
6. Bake uncovered for 25 minutes or until they are no longer pink inside.

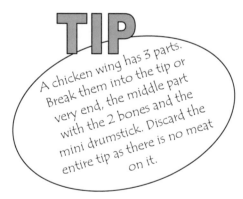

TIP

A chicken wing has 3 parts. Break them into the tip or very end, the middle part with the 2 bones and the mini drumstick. Discard the entire tip as there is no meat on it.

Cookie sheet

Small bowl

Mayda C's Chinese Lettuce Wraps

1/2 pound of boneless, skinless chicken breasts cut into 1/2 inch strips
1/4 cup cashew or peanut pieces (found in the baking aisle)
1/4 cup grated carrots (found in the produce section)
1 can sliced water chestnuts
1 head iceberg lettuce
1 cup teriyaki sauce
canola cooking spray

TIP

An easy way to dry lettuce leaves is to individually place them on a terry towel, roll the towel up (jelly roll fashion) and put it in the refrigerator for a while. The towel absorbs the water and leaves the lettuce fresh and dry.

1. Wash the lettuce and let it dry completely.
2. Spray a medium skillet with cooking spray and heat over medium low heat.
3. Cook the chicken until no longer pink (about 4 minutes each side).
4. Drain the water chestnuts (discard the liquid) and add them to the skillet. Add cashews and carrots and continue cooking on low heat until warm (about 3 minutes).
5. 5. Add the teriyaki sauce to the skillet and stir it all together.
6. To serve separate lettuce leafs. Spoon a small amount of chicken mixture onto the lettuce leaves and fold.

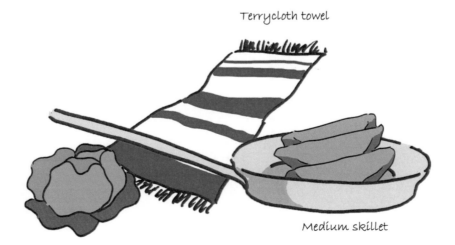

Terrycloth towel

Medium skillet

dinner

entree

spread

main course

feast

supper

Sharon S's Absolutely Fantastic Apricot Chicken

2 or 3 boneless, skinless, chicken breasts
1/3 cup apricot jam (or your favorite flavor)
1 envelope onion soup mix
1/4 teaspoon lemon juice
1/4 cup bottled italian dressing

Preheat oven to 350°

1. Mix all the ingredients except the chicken in a small bowl to make the marinade.
2. Place the chicken in a plastic bag and pour the marinade in the plastic bag. Let the chicken marinate overnight in the refrigerator.
3. Remove the chicken from bag, discard leftover marinade and the bag. Bake the chicken in a small baking pan uncovered for about 45 minutes.
4. The chicken is done when you pierce the chicken with a fork, juices are clear and inside is not pink.

TIP
You can substitute chicken bone-in parts. Cooking times may have to be increased slightly.

TIP
Chicken is done when it registers 165° for breast and 170° for thighs, when a meat thermometer is placed in the thickest part of the chicken.

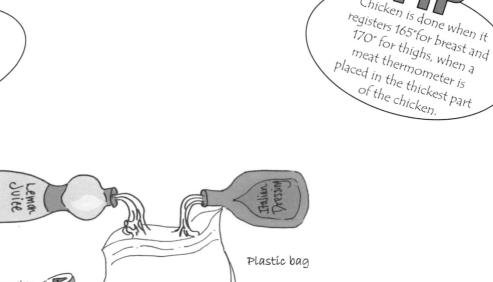

Lemon Juice

Italian Dressing

Plastic bag

Meat thermometer

Small bowl

Small baking pan

Michelle W's We Love It Peanut Chicken

2 boneless, skinless chicken breasts cut into 2 inch strips
1 teaspoon sesame oil
1 teaspoon soy sauce
1 teaspoon fresh minced garlic
1/4 cup creamy style peanut butter
2 tablespoons rice vinegar
1 teaspoon canola oil

1. In a medium bowl combine the sesame oil, soy sauce and garlic.
2. Add the chicken to the bowl.
3. Heat a grill pan over high heat. Brush the pan with oil.
4. Remove the chicken from the bowl and discard any remaining sauce.
5. Cook the chicken until it is no longer pink inside (about 6 minutes each side.)
6. In a small bowl mix the peanut butter, vinegar and 2-3 tablespoons of water to make a dipping sauce. Blend until smooth.
7. Serve the chicken with the dipping sauce.

TIP

A grill pan is a heavy metal pan that has ridges. They can be found in varying shapes and are used to simulate the grilling process.

TIP

If you buy organic peanut butter, and the oil separates, turn the jar upside down overnight. Gravity will recombine it in. Store it in the refrigerator for freshness.

Grill pan

Medium bowl

Small bowl

Cheryl S's Banner Baked Oniony Chicken

1/4 cup olive oil
1 envelope onion soup mix
1 large yellow onion sliced in 1/4 inch rounds
4 pieces of chicken with bone and skin, cut into eighths
1/2 teaspoon hungarian paprika
canola cooking spray

Preheat oven to 375°

1. Spray a medium baking pan with cooking spray.
2. Put 1/2 of the onion soup in bottom of the prepared pan and set aside.
3. In a medium bowl mix olive oil, remaining onion soup mix and onions.
4. Place the chicken in pan and cover with onion mixture. Sprinkle with paprika.
5. Bake uncovered for 1 hour or until chicken is brown.

TIP

Using olive oil in your diet increases the amount of mono-saturated fats which are healthier.

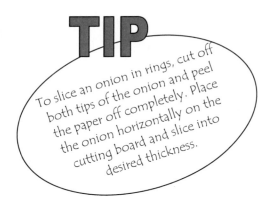

TIP

To slice an onion in rings, cut off both tips of the onion and peel the paper off completely. Place the onion horizontally on the cutting board and slice into desired thickness.

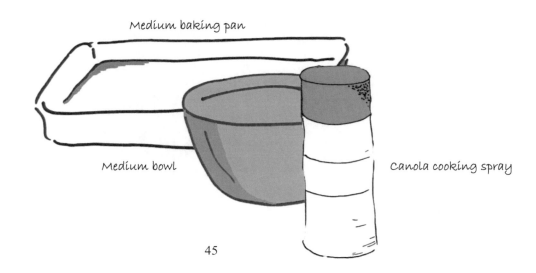

Medium baking pan

Medium bowl

Canola cooking spray

Emily L's Laden Chicken With Peaches

3/4 cup peach preserves
1 tablespoon honey
1/2 tablespoon dijon mustard
2 boneless, skinless chicken breasts cut into 2 inch strips
2 fresh peaches sliced in thin slices

1. In a large nonstick skillet cook the preserves, honey and mustard, stirring over medium low heat.
2. Add the chicken and cook it turning frequently until cooked through (about 15 minutes or until it is no longer pink).
3. Add the sliced peaches to the chicken.
4. Cook for additional 5 minutes over low heat.

TIP
Peach flesh tends to turn brown when exposed to the air. To avoid this, sprinkle with lemon juice.

TIP
To pick peaches they should be firm and free of bruises. A ripe peach tends to be heavy and larger.

Cutting board

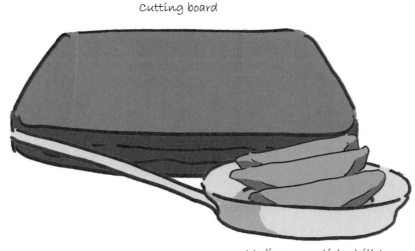

Medium nonstick skillet

Caren B's Capellini, Chicken And Sun-Dried Tomatoes

2 boneless, skinless chicken breasts cut into 2 inch strips
4 ounces angel hair pasta
1 tablespoon olive oil
1 teaspoon fresh minced garlic
1/2 cup sun-dried tomatoes not packed in oil (found in the produce section)

1.   Boil water in a medium saucepan and cook pasta following package directions.
2.   Soak the sun-dried tomatoes in hot water in a small bowl for 10 minutes until soft.
3.   Drain the tomatoes and chop into small pieces (keep the water from the tomatoes).
4.   Heat the oil in a medium skillet over medium high heat.
5.   Add the chicken and garlic to the skillet and cook until the garlic turns golden brown.
6.   Stir in the soaked sun-dried tomatoes and the reserved water. Continue cooking until the chicken is no longer pink.
7. Lower heat to medium, add cooked pasta to the skillet and continue cooking for a few minutes until the pasta is cooked through.

TIP
Do not stir the pasta in the first few minutes of cooking. This avoids the pasta strands from sticking together.

TIP
You can add a very small amount of oil to the pot before cooking pasta, or oil the bottom of the pot and swirl it around before you put the water in to avoid the pasta from sticking to the pot.

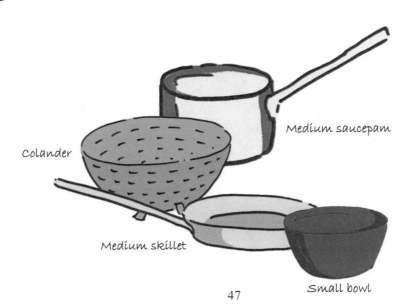

Colander

Medium saucepam

Medium skillet

Small bowl

Lynn D's Coconut Chicken

4 tablespoons unsalted butter or margarine
3/4 cup panko breadcrumbs
1/4 cup unsweetened shredded coconut
3/4 pound boneless, skinless chicken breasts cut into 2 inch strips
canola cooking spray

Preheat oven to 400°

1. Spray a rimmed cookie sheet with cooking spray.
2. Melt the butter or margarine in a small microwaveable bowl (see tip).
3. Combine breadcrumbs and coconut in a plastic bag.
4. Dip the chicken in the melted butter and then place it in the plastic bag. Evenly coat the chicken with the coconut breadcrumb mixture.
5. Remove the chicken from the bag. Discard the bag and remaining breadcrumb mixture. Place the chicken on the prepared cookie sheet and bake uncovered until crisp or golden brown for about 25 minutes.

TIP
You can buy chicken tenders already cut up.

TIP
Butter melts very quickly in the microwave. Cut the butter into small cubes and melt for about 15-20 seconds.

TIP
When melting butter, cover bowl with a paper towel to avoid splattering.

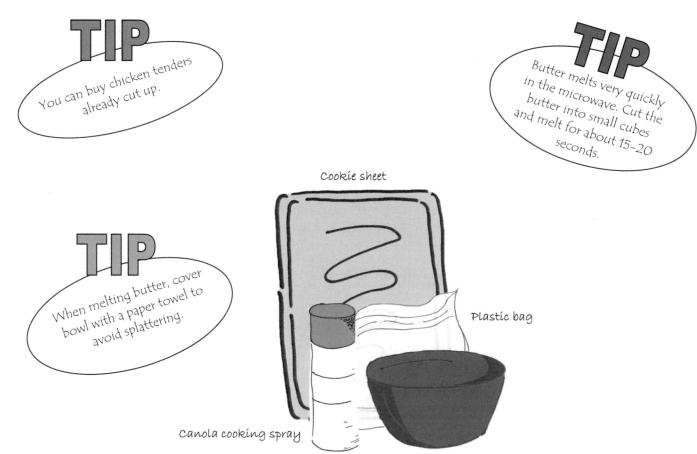

Cookie sheet

Plastic bag

Canola cooking spray

Small bowl

Anne R's Cola Chicken

2 yellow onions sliced in 1/4 inch rounds
4 pieces chicken with bone and skin, cut into eighths
1/2 cup cola
1/4 cup ketchup
1/4 cup apricot preserves or jelly
1/2 tablespoon soy sauce
canola cooking spray

Preheat oven to 375°

1. Spray a medium baking pan with cooking spray.
2. Arrange sliced onions in a single layer in the baking pan.
3. Mix cola, ketchup, apricot preserves and soy sauce in a medium bowl.
4. Add the chicken to the bowl and toss with sauce.
5. Remove the chicken from the bowl and place it on top of the onions in the prepared pan.
6. Bake, uncovered for about 1 hour or until chicken is no longer pink.

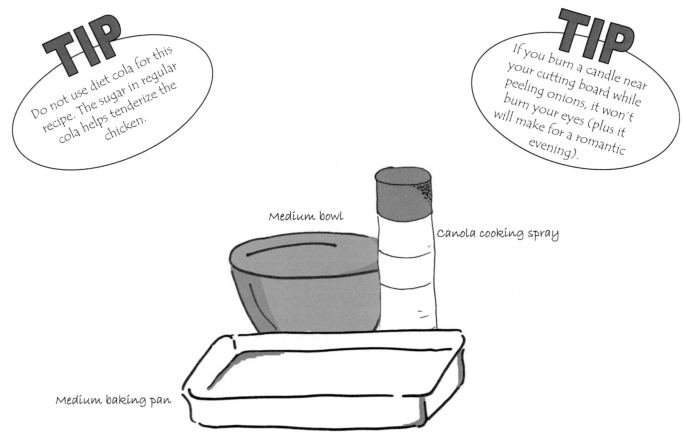

TIP
Do not use diet cola for this recipe. The sugar in regular cola helps tenderize the chicken.

TIP
If you burn a candle near your cutting board while peeling onions, it won't burn your eyes (plus it will make for a romantic evening).

Medium bowl

Canola cooking spray

Medium baking pan

Margery Ann R's Really Mustardy And Honey Chicken

1/8 cup dijon mustard
2 tablespoons honey
1 teaspoon lemon juice
1/2 cup plain breadcrumbs
2 large boneless, skinless chicken breasts
1 tablespoon olive oil
canola cooking spray

TIP
You can also use seasoned breadcrumbs for more flavor.

Heat oven to 375°

1. Lightly grease a rimmed cookie sheet with cooking spray or a paper towel dipped in olive oil.
2. Mix the mustard, honey and lemon juice in a small bowl.
3. Place the breadcrumbs in a second bowl.
4. Dip the chicken breasts in honey mustard mixture and coat well.
5. Dip the chicken in the breadcrumbs covering them completely.
6. Place on the prepared cookie sheet and sprinkle the chicken with olive oil.
7. Bake for 20-25 minutes or until chicken is no longer pink inside.

TIP
Store breadcrumbs in the freezer to maintain freshness.

Cookie sheet

Canola cooking spray

Small bowls

50

Janet Z's Kool Krunchy Chicken

1 cup "French's Fried Onions"
1 tablespoon all purpose flour
2 boneless, skinless chicken breasts cut into 1 inch strips
1 egg
canola cooking spray

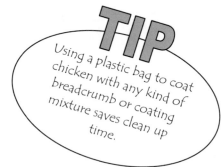

TIP
Using a plastic bag to coat chicken with any kind of breadcrumb or coating mixture saves clean up time.

Preheat oven to 400°

1. Spray a rimmed cookie sheet with cooking spray.
2. Beat the egg in a small bowl and set aside.
3. Pour the flour and fried onions in a plastic bag. Crush to make crumbs.
4. Dip each piece of chicken in the egg and then put in the plastic bag to coat with crumbs.
5. As you remove each piece of chicken from the bag place it on the prepared cookie sheet.
6. When they have all been coated with the egg and crumb mixture, bake uncovered for 10 minutes or until the chicken is no longer pink inside.

TIP
Use ketchup, duck sauce or barbeque sauce on the side when serving.

TIP
Use a pitcher for flowers for a pretty centerpiece.

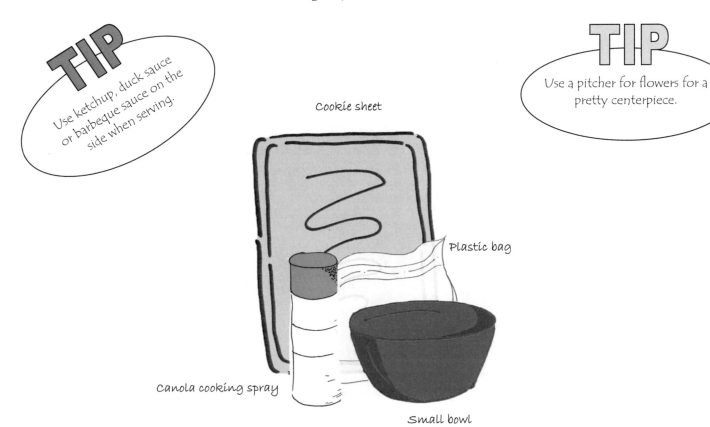

Cookie sheet

Plastic bag

Canola cooking spray

Small bowl

Robin L's Kan't Leave Without It Kahlua Chicken

1/2 cup kahlua
1/4 cup chili sauce
2 tablespoons pineapple juice
1 tablespoon cornstarch
1/2 pound boneless, skinless chicken breasts

1. Combine the kahlua, chili sauce and pineapple juice in a medium saucepan.
2. Mix the cornstarch in a small bowl with a little bit of water to make a thin paste.
3. Warm the kahlua mixture over a low heat and add in the cornstarch paste slowly.
4. Bring to a boil (so cornstarch paste will start to thicken, then lower heat). Stir the mixture until it thickens.
5. Baste the chicken with the sauce and barbeque over low coals for about 30-40 minutes until juices run clear.

TIP
This sauce can be used for ribs, chicken legs or chicken breasts with the bone.

TIP
You can pour the barbeque sauce over chicken in a baking dish and bake at 350° for 30-40 minutes.

Grill

Medium saucepan

Small bowl

Brush

Lila S's Extra Easy Baked Chicken

1/4 cup all purpose flour
1/4 cup extra virgin olive oil
1/2 tablespoon hungarian paprika
1/2 cup water
1/2 cup ketchup
1 small yellow onion, chopped in 1 inch pieces
1/2 teaspoon minced garlic
1 pound chicken parts (white or dark or combination of both), with bone and skin, cut into eighths
canola cooking spray

TIP
Hungarian paprika is found in the spice aisle and gives the chicken a wonderful color.

Heat oven to 325°

1. Spray a medium baking pan with cooking spray.
2. Arrange the chicken in the pan.
3. Mix the flour, oil, and paprika to make a paste in a small bowl.
4. Coat the chicken with the paste.
5. Combine the water, ketchup, onion and garlic in a small saucepan. Bring it to a boil.
6. Pour this mixture over chicken and bake uncovered until tender about 1 hour.

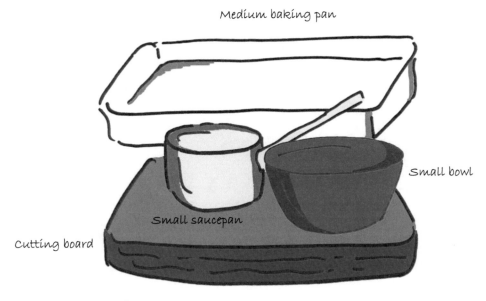

Medium baking pan

Small bowl

Small saucepan

Cutting board

Jeri P's Magical Mustard Chicken

2 tablespoons dijon mustard
2 tablespoons water
1 teaspoon garlic powder
1/4 teaspoon italian seasoning
2 boneless, skinless chicken breasts

Preheat oven to 375°

1. Mix the mustard, water, garlic powder and italian seasoning in a plastic bag.
2. Add the chicken and coat well. Remove the chicken, discard the bag and remaining marinade.
3. Place the chicken in a small baking pan and bake uncovered for 20 minutes or until it is no longer pink inside.

TIP

This dish goes well with yellow or brown rice..

TIP

Italian seasoning is a wonderful blend of dried basil, oregano and thyme. It can also be used to make great garlic bread.

Plastic bag

Small baking pan

Lynny R's Cheesy Chicken Cheese Casserole

TIP
Try different kinds of pasta sauce like Alfredo or Vodka to change this up a little.

olive oil
2 thin boneless, skinless chicken breasts
1 cup pasta sauce
2 cups multi-cheese mozzarella, romano, cheddar mix
(comes in a bag in cheese aisle)
1 cup seasoned or plain breadcrumbs
1 teaspoon garlic powder
canola cooking spray

Preheat oven to 400°

1. Spray a small baking pan with cooking spray.
2. Put the chicken breasts on the bottom of pan.
3. Sprinkle them with breadcrumbs.
4. Sprinkle them with garlic powder.
5. Cover them with the pasta sauce.
6. Sprinkle the cheese on top.
7. Cover with aluminum foil and bake for 30 minutes or until the chicken is no longer pink inside.

TIP
Try planting herbs in a basket or attractive container. You can always use it for a centerpiece.

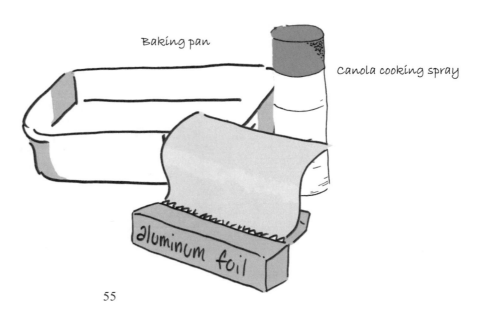

Baking pan

Canola cooking spray

aluminum foil

Terry B's Best Broccoli Chicken Dinner

4 boneless, skinless chicken breasts
1 package of frozen broccoli
1-2 cups cooked instant rice
1 cup white wine
1 tablespoon olive oil
2-3 tablespoons of dijon mustard
4 slices of mozzarella or cheese of choice

TIP
To defrost broccoli, place it in a colander and rinse with warm water for about 1 minute. Drain well and press out extra water.

1. Defrost box of frozen broccoli. Do not cook it. Set it aside.
2. Heat the olive oil in a medium skillet.
3. Brown the chicken in the skillet over medium low heat for about 5-10 minutes. Check that the chicken is not pink inside.
4. Add the broccoli and continue cooking for another 2 minutes together. Add the wine.
5. Prepare the rice according to directions in a medium pot. Set aside.
6. Spread the mustard on the chicken and add cooked rice to the skillet.
7. Place the cheese on top of the chicken. Cover the pan and continue cooking to melt the cheese for about 2 more minutes.

TIP
You can substitute fresh broccoli .

Medium pot

Colander

Medium Skillet

Karin E's Red Wine Chicken

2 chicken breasts with bone and skin
1/2 tablespoon olive oil
1 tablespoon fresh minced garlic
1/2 tablespoon hungarian paprika
1/2 cup red wine
1/2 cup brown sugar
salt and black pepper

Preheat oven to 350°

TIP

Fruity red or white wine compliments any chicken dish.

1. Place chicken in a small baking pan.
2. Mix all the other ingredients in a small bowl to make a sauce.
3. Pour the sauce over the chicken and bake uncovered for 45 minutes or until no longer pink.

TIP

Use ice cubes and a pinch of baking soda in your garbage disposal to help get rid of built up grease and remove any smell. Remember to always run the water when using your disposal.

TIP

Let your favorite, most expensive wine rest on it's side in a cool, dark place for a month to truly enjoy the flavor.

Small bowl

Small baking pan

Reeta W's Rockin' Roasted Maple Chicken

1 small yellow onion sliced in 1/4 inch rounds
2 tablespoons olive oil
4 pieces chicken with bone and skin, cut into eighths
3 tablespoons maple syrup
salt and black pepper

TIP

Always wash your hands and utensils well with warm soapy water when handling raw chicken to avoid contamination.

Preheat oven to 400°

1. Season the chicken with a dash of salt and pepper.
2. Arrange the onions in a single layer in a medium baking pan and drizzle with olive oil.
3. Put the chicken on top of the onions and pour maple syrup over chicken.
4. Bake the chicken uncovered until it is no longer pink; for about 45 minutes.

TIP

Plastic cutting boards are great for trimming raw chicken so they can be washed in the dishwasher or washed by hand in warm, soapy water.

Medium baking pan

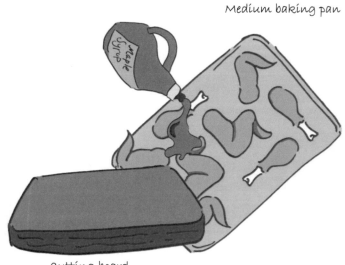

Cutting board

Karyn W's Way To Go Noodles And Cheese

1/2 package of egg noodles (6-8 ounces)
1 teaspoon olive oil
1/2 pound lean ground beef
1 small yellow onion chopped in 1/4 inch pieces
1 can tomato soup (the kind you add water to) (10 ounces)
1/3 cup water
1/4 cup shredded mozzarella cheese

Heat oven to 350°

TIP

When browning ground beef always make sure the pan is hot enough, there is sufficient oil in the pan and the meat is not overcrowded. This will help to evenly brown the contents and not stick to the pan.

1. Cook the noodles according to package directions in a large saucepan. Drain them in a colander and set aside.
2. Heat the oil on medium high in a medium skillet. Add the ground beef and chopped onion.
3. Continue cooking over medium high heat until the meat is no longer pink.
4. Drain off any fat by holding a spoon at edge of skillet and tilting it to allow the fat to pour out (if you have a strainer, you can add the contents of the pan to the strainer and just press down on the meat with a large spoon and allow the grease to drip through the strainer).
5. In a medium baking pan mix the drained meat, cooked noodles, 1/3 cup water, tomato soup and 1/2 of the cheese.
6. Sprinkle the remaining cheese on top of the meat mixture.
7. Bake uncovered for 25-30 minutes.

TIP

When sautéing or browning, heat the pan first and then add your oil or butter to allow the fat to get hotter faster.

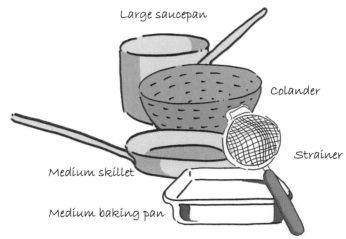

Large saucepan

Colander

Strainer

Medium skillet

Medium baking pan

Flossie F's Easy Meatloaf

1 egg, beaten
1/2 cup pasta sauce
1/4 cup breadcrumbs
1/2 pound lean ground beef
1/2 cup shredded mozzarella cheese
salt (optional)

Preheat oven to 450°

1. In a medium bowl combine the egg, 1/4 cup pasta sauce, breadcrumbs and a dash of salt.
2. Add the beef and 1/4 cup of the cheese.
3. Mix well.
4. Divide the meat mixture into 2 equal portions and shape each one into a mini loaf.
5. Place the loaves on a rimmed cookie sheet.
6. Spoon the remaining pasta sauce on the loaves and sprinkle with the remaining cheese.
7. Bake uncovered about 15 minutes or until the meat is no longer pink inside.

TIP
You can substitute ground turkey or chicken or a combination of meats and poultry for a healthy alternative.

Cookie sheet

Medium bowl

Mothers Of Sons Meatballs

1 package of pre-made cooked turkey meatballs
(available either frozen or in the meat department)
1 bottle chili sauce (12 ounces) (found near the ketchup)
1 can whole berry or jellied cranberry sauce (14 ounces)
12 ginger snap cookies
1/2 cup water

1. Mix the chili sauce, cranberry sauce and 2 cups of water in a large pot with a cover
(break up any large pieces of cranberry sauce with the back of the spoon).
2. Crush the ginger snap cookies, and add them to the pot and stir.
3. Drop the meatballs into the pot and gently stir so they are covered well with the sauce.
4. Cover the pot and cook over medium low heat for about 20 minutes just before the
sauce begins to boil.

TIP
This recipe won 1st place in a cooking contest.

TIP
Serve over rice, noodles, couscous or quinoa or as an appetizer on toothpicks.

TIP
Using the jellied sauce and 1/8 teaspoon of ginger powder or fresh minced ginger instead of the ginger snap cookies creates a smoother, less lumpy sauce.

Large pot with cover

Lois F's Chow Down Chili

1 teaspoons olive oil
1 pound lean ground beef
1 small yellow onion chopped in 1/4 inch pieces
1 can diced tomatoes (14 1/2 ounces)
1 can tomato paste (6 ounces)
1/2 cup water
1 tablespoon sugar
1 can of kidney beans (15 ounces)
1/4 –1/2 tablespoon chili powder

1. Drain and rinse the kidney beans in a colander and set them aside.
2. Heat the oil on medium high in a large skillet that has a cover. Add the ground beef and chopped onion to the pan.
3. Continue cooking over medium high heat until the meat is no longer pink.
4. Drain the fat off.
5. Add the diced tomatoes with the liquid and all the other ingredients except for the chili powder.
6. Add the chili powder tasting it as you do to determine if it is seasoned as you like.
7. Bring to a boil over medium high heat, reduce the heat to low, cover and simmer for about 15 minutes or till most of the liquid is absorbed.

TIP
If chili is too thick, use beef broth to dilute it.

TIP
If chili is too thin, add tomato paste to thicken it.

Colander

Large skillet

Penny F's Luscious Lasagna And Broccoli Bake

1 cup part-skim ricotta cheese
1 cup cottage cheese
2 cups shredded mozzarella cheese
2 eggs, beaten
1 small package frozen broccoli (10 ounces)
1 package no-boil lasagna noodles (9 ounces)
1 jar of your favorite pasta sauce (32 ounces)
canola cooking spray

TIP
No-boil lasagna noodles are in the pasta aisle and are a great time saving ingredient.

Preheat oven to 400°

1. Defrost the broccoli in the refrigerator or in the sink and squeeze to get all the water out.
2. Spray a 13 x 9 baking pan with cooking spray.
3. Combine the ricotta and cottage cheese, 1 cup of mozzarella cheese, eggs and broccoli in a large bowl.
4. Pour a little pasta sauce in the bottom of the baking pan.
5. Place 3 of the lasagna noodles in the baking pan.
6. Spread 1/3 of cheese mixture evenly over the noodles.
7. Pour 1/3 of pasta sauce on top.
8. Repeat this process 2 more times.
9. Sprinkle with the remaining mozzarella cheese on top.
10. Bake uncovered for 30 minutes or till bubbling.
11. Let stand 10 minutes before serving.

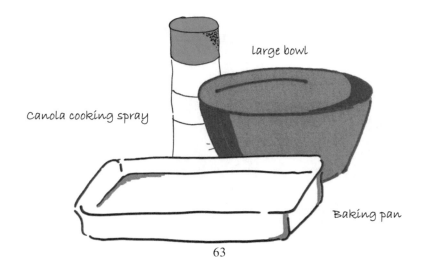

large bowl

Canola cooking spray

Baking pan

Laura G's Brisket With Ketchup And Ginger Ale

4 yellow onions sliced in 1/4 inch rounds
1 pound brisket of beef
1 cup ketchup
1 envelope onion soup mix
ginger ale (12 ounce bottle)
1/2 cup red wine

1. Arrange the onions in the bottom of a large dutch oven pot.
2. Place the brisket on top of the onions.
3. Add the ketchup, soup mix, ginger ale and wine to the pot.
4. Cook on top of the stove at medium heat for 2-2 1/2 hours or until the brisket is tender with a fork.
5. Cool it and slice against the grain.

TIP
This serves more than two. Freeze the rest and enjoy a meal again.

TIP
Brisket always tastes better the day after you cook it.

TIP
A large dutch oven pot can be used for soup or making pasta in addition to the brisket.

Dutch oven

Bobbi B's Better The Next Day Brisket

TIP

Slice the brisket when cold, it makes it easier to slice thin and to trim off all the fat.

1 1/2 pound beef brisket
1 medium onion sliced in 1/4 inch rings
1 teaspoon fresh minced garlic
1 teaspoon hungarian paprika
1/2 cup apricot preserves or jelly
1/2 teaspoon lemon juice
1 can cola (12 ounces)
canola cooking spray

Preheat oven to 325°

1. Spray a large baking pan with canola cooking spray.
2. Arrange the onions in a single layer in the bottom of pan.
3. Put the brisket on top of the onions.
4. In a small bowl mix ,minced garlic, paprika and apricot preserves or jelly and coat both sides of brisket with the mixture.
5. Pour lemon juice and cola over brisket.
6. Let stand for 1 hour at room temperature.
7. Bake covered about 2 hours or until tender and easy to slice.

TIP

Always cut brisket against the grain.

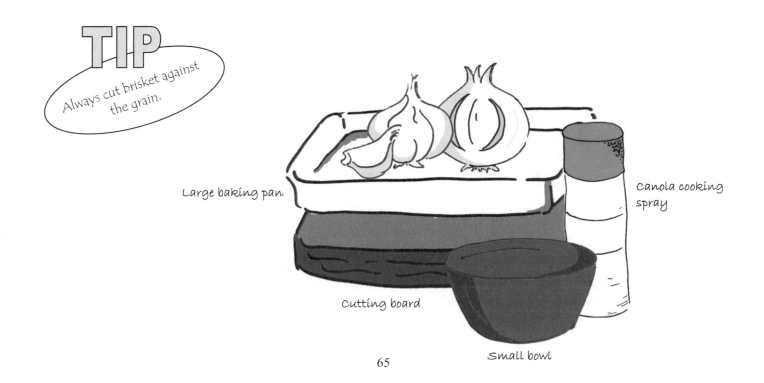

Large baking pan

Canola cooking spray

Cutting board

Small bowl

Andrea K's Kook On The Grill Pan Flank Steak

1/8 cup soy sauce
1/8 cup olive oil
1 tablespoon lemon juice
1 tablespoon fresh minced garlic
3 scallions white and green parts chopped in 1/4 inch pieces
1 pound flank steak

TIP
To stop scallions from rolling off the cutting board, cut a slit down the center lengthwise and then start chopping.

1. Add soy sauce, oil, lemon juice, garlic and scallions in a small bowl.
2. Place the steak in a plastic bag with the marinade and put it in the refrigerator for 3 hours to overnight.
3. Pre-heat the grill.
4. Remove the steak from the bag and discard the bag and remaining marinade.
5. Let the steak stand at room temperature for 20 minutes before grilling.
6. Grill to desired doneness.

Grill

Plastic bag

Skillet

Small bowl

Nancy M's Mouth Watering Flank Steak

TIP
Always discard leftover marinade.

1/4 cup soy sauce
3 tablespoons honey
2 tablespoons white vinegar
1 1/2 teaspoons garlic powder
1 1/2 teaspoons ground ginger powder
3/4 cup canola oil
1 individual scallion, chopped in 1/4 inch pieces
1 flank steak or london broil about 1 1/2 pounds

1. Mix together the soy sauce, honey and vinegar in a small bowl.
2. Blend in the garlic powder, ginger, oil and chopped scallion.
3. Put the meat in a large plastic bag, add marinade and place tightly closed bag in the refrigerator for 1 hour to overnight.
4. Remove the bag from the refrigerator 1/2 hour before cooking and discard the bag and the marinade.
5. Cook over a hot grill, grill pan or broiler for about 5 minutes each side (for medium rare) or until the steak is to your liking.
6. Slice the meat against the grain.
7. Let the steak rest for a few minutes before serving.

TIP
The longer you leave meat to marinate, the better the flavor.

Grill pan

Small bowl

Plastic bag

Cutting board

Adele B's Impress Your Date Steak Sandwiches

TIP
Boursin cheese is similar to cream cheese and is available in different flavors. Any are suitable for this recipe.

1 flank steak (16 ounces)
2 fresh steak or hoagie rolls
1 package herb boursin cheese (5.2 ounces)
1 tablespoon olive oil
salt and black pepper
few romaine lettuce leaves

1. Preheat the broiler, grill pan or indoor grill.
2. Pat the steak dry and season with a little salt and pepper.
3. Broil the steak on the rack of broiler pan, grill or grill pan 6-8 minutes each side for medium rare.
4. While the steak is broiling cut the rolls in half and spread the bottom halves with cheese.
5. Transfer the steak to a cutting board and let it stand for a few minutes.
6. In a small skillet heat the oil over slightly high heat until hot but not smoking.
7. Cook the lettuce until it is slightly wilted for a few minutes.
8. Slice the steak across the grain.
9. Place the lettuce on the rolls on top of the cheese and add the steak to assemble sandwiches.

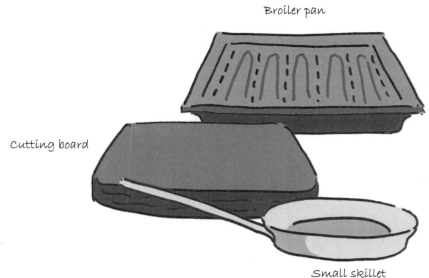

Broiler pan

Cutting board

Small skillet

Audrey Y's Best Beef Burgundy

1 can cream of mushroom soup
1 envelope onion soup mix
1 1/2 cups burgundy wine
1/2 pound boneless sirloin steak cut into cubes
1 large yellow onion chopped in 1 inch pieces

1. Combine mushroom soup, onion soup mix, and wine in a microwaveable dish that has a cover.
2. Add the beef and onion, mix well and cover.
3. Microwave on High for about 10-12 minutes or until boiling.
4. Stir well and cover again.
5. Microwave on Medium for about 45-55 minutes until tender.

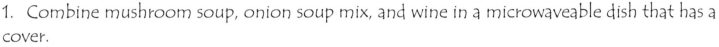

TIP
If you don't have a cover for the casserole you can use plastic wrap.

TIP
Serve over cooked noodles or rice.

TIP
Never use anything made of metal in the microwave.

Microwaveable dish

Cutting board

Cindy F's Panko Pork Chops

1 1/2 cups panko (japanese breadcrumbs)
2 tablespoons olive oil
2 boneless pork loin chops (6-8 ounces each)
2 tablespoons dijon mustard
salt and pepper

Preheat oven to 425°

1. Pour oil onto a rimmed cookie sheet, add Panko breadcrumbs and stir them around until they are well coated with oil.
2. Bake until golden brown, 7-10 minutes.
3. Transfer to a medium bowl.
4. Reduce oven temperature to 400°.
5. One at a time, place the chops between two large pieces of plastic wrap. Using a meat mallet or the bottom of a small heavy pan, pound them to make 1/4 inch thick cutlets.
6. Coat the pork chops with mustard (use a brush or knife). Season with salt and pepper.
7. Dip each cutlet into the panko, pressing firmly so the breadcrumbs stick to the pork chops.
8. Place a rack on the rimmed cookie sheet; place the chops on rack, and bake uncovered, without turning, until opaque throughout, 10-15 minutes.

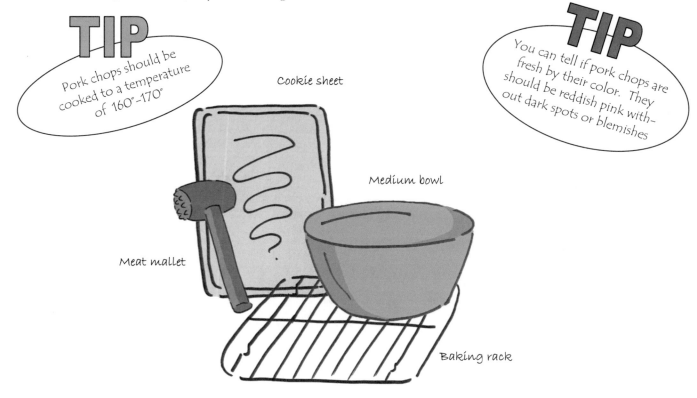

TIP
Pork chops should be cooked to a temperature of 160°-170°

Cookie sheet

TIP
You can tell if pork chops are fresh by their color. They should be reddish pink with-out dark spots or blemishes

Medium bowl

Meat mallet

Baking rack

Terri W's Terrific Teriyaki Pork Chops

2 boneless pork chops
1/4 cup teriyaki sauce
1/2 tablespoon sugar
1 tablespoon pineapple juice

TIP
This marinade can be used for chicken as well as pork.

1. Rinse the pork chops and dry them well.
2. Put the pork chops in a plastic bag.
3. Combine the teriyaki sauce, sugar and pineapple juice in a small bowl and mix well to make the marinade.
4. Pour the marinade into the plastic bag.
5. Refrigerate the chops in the bag for 4-6 hours.
6. Remove the pork from the marinade and discard leftover marinade and the bag.
7. Heat a grill pan or indoor grill and grill until they are not pink about 8-12 minutes.

TIP
To keep this cookbook flat, stick several coins between 2 pieces of duct tape, stick them together and use it as a paperweight to keep the pages open.

TIP
To save clean-up time, mix the marinade right in the plastic bag.

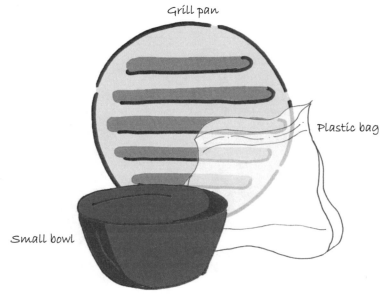

Grill pan

Plastic bag

Small bowl

Sandi L's Tomatoey Turkey Casserole

2 tablespoons canola oil
1 pound ground turkey
1/2 yellow onion sliced in 1/4 inch rounds
3 teaspoons fresh minced garlic
1 large can diced tomatoes (28 ounces)
1 cup grated parmesan cheese
salt and black pepper

1. In a large skillet, heat the oil over medium high heat.
2. Mix the turkey, onion, and garlic in a medium bowl and add to the skillet.
3. Cook until the turkey is browned, and the onion is tender.
4. Drain the tomatoes with a slotted spoon and add them to skillet. Discard the liquid.
5. Season with a pinch of salt and black pepper.
6. Simmer on low heat for about 15 minutes.
7. Put the turkey in a serving dish and sprinkle with grated cheese.

TIP
Serve this over pasta for a quick complete dinner.

TIP
Ground turkey is lower in fat and healthier than ground beef.

Medium bowl

Slotted spoon

large skillet

Bette F's Bungalow Barbecued Hot Dogs

4 hot dogs
1 yellow onion sliced in 1/4 inch rounds
1/2 teaspoon extra virgin olive oil
1 teaspoon sugar
1/2 teaspoon dry mustard
1/2 teaspoon hungarian paprika
2 tablespoons white vinegar
1/4 cup ketchup
1/4 cup water

TIP
Basting helps meat and poultry preserve moisture and adds flavor.

Heat oven to 350°

1. Split hot dogs in half lengthwise, flip them and place in baking pan cut side down.
2. Heat the olive oil in a medium saucepan on medium heat.
3. Cook the onions in the medium saucepan until brown.
4. Add the remaining ingredients except for the hot dogs and simmer for 15 minutes to make the barbecue sauce.
5. Pour the sauce over hot dogs.
6. Bake for about 15 minutes basting frequently.

TIP
You can use deli mustard instead of dry mustard.

TIP
Basting is taking the sauce with a spoon or brush and covering the franks with it about every 5 minutes.

Baking pan

Medium Saucepan

Cutting board

73

Marilyn H's Hearty Mushroom Pot Roast

1 can cream of mushroom soup
1 envelope onion soup mix
6 small red potatoes cut in half
6 medium carrots cut into 2 inch pieces
1 3 pound beef chuck pot roast or boneless bottom round

1. Put the canned soup, soup mix, potatoes and carrots into your crockpot.
2. Add the beef and flip it a few times to cover it with the onion soup and mushroom soup mixture.
3. Cover the crockpot and cook on low for 8-9 hours (on high about 5-6 hrs) or until the beef is fork tender.

TIP

One hour on high equals 2 hours on low in the crockpot.

TIP

Do not open the crockpot to check on your dinner. This allows heat to escape and you may need to increase cooking time.

Crockpot

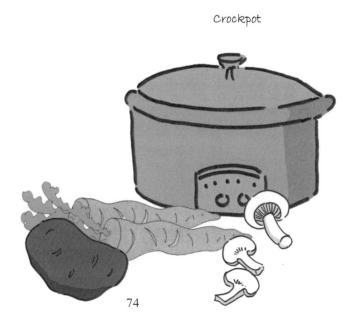

Liz G's 3-Step Spareribs

1 small bottle of your favorite barbecue sauce (18 ounces)
1 pound pork or beef spareribs cut individually

1. Place the ribs in your crockpot.
2. Cover them with the barbecue sauce
3. Cook on low for 8-10 hours.

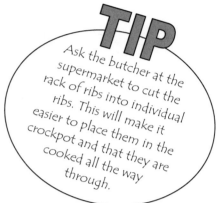

TIP Ask the butcher at the supermarket to cut the rack of ribs into individual ribs. This will make it easier to place them in the crockpot and that they are cooked all the way through.

TIP Remove the white membrane from the rack of ribs before cooking it. This will help make them tender and juicy. Cut a slit in it with a sharp, small knife and use your fingers to pull it off each rib until the end of the rack.

TIP Only fill a crockpot 1/2 to 2/3 full. Food will not cook properly if filled to the top.

TIP Try to purchase a crockpot with a removable liner. If you don't have one, you can always line it with a cooking bag. This will make cleanup much easier.

Crockpot

Laureen S's Slow Cooker Chicken Alfredo

4 boneless, skinless chicken breasts
1/4 cup water
1 package of Italian salad dressing
(found in the salad dressing aisle)
1 teaspoon minced fresh garlic
1 package cream cheese (8 ounces)
1 can cream of chicken soup (10 3/4ounces)
canola cooking spray

TIP

A crockpot is great for cooking when you work. Get the dish going in the morning, set the crockpot and by the time you get home from work dinner is waiting for you.

1. Spray the inside of the crock pot with cooking spray.
2. Put the chicken breasts in the crockpot.
3. Mix the italian dressing with water in a small bowl, add the garlic and pour over the chicken in the crockpot.
4. Cover the crockpot and cook on low setting for 4 hours.
5. After 4 hours soften the cream cheese (see tip) and mix it with the cream of chicken soup in a small bowl. Add to the crockpot.
6. Cover and cook for another hour.

TIP

To soften the cream cheese, place it in a plastic bag and immerse it in hot water. It will be soft in a short time.

Crockpot

Small bowl

Leslie K's Perfect Poached Fish

2 frozen fish fillets, defrosted
1/4 cup dry white wine
Salt and black pepper

Makes 2 servings

TIP
Put a few lemon slices in a bowl of water and cook in the microwave to remove any fish smell after cooking fish.

1. Place the fillets in a small glass baking dish.
2. Pour the wine over the fish fillets.
3. Sprinkle them with salt and pepper.
4. Cover the dish with paper towels and cook in the microwave at Medium High for about 5 minutes.
5. The fish will be done when it flakes easily with a fork.

TIP
Salmon, trout, tilapia, cod, sole, haddock, snapper or halibut can be used in this recipe.

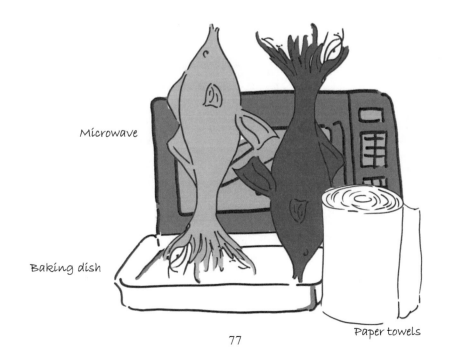

Microwave

Baking dish

Paper towels

Debbie O's Shrimp Scampi

1/4 cup butter or margarine
1 teaspoon fresh minced garlic
2 tablespoons lemon juice
1 pound frozen shrimp, defrosted, shelled and deveined
hungarian paprika

1. Place the butter and garlic in a medium glass casserole.
2. Microwave on High for about 1 minute until the butter or margarine is melted and the garlic begins to soften.
3. Add the shrimp and stir in lemon juice (make sure the shrimp is coated with the sauce).
4. Cover the casserole loosely with paper towels.
5. Microwave at Medium High for about 5 minutes stirring a few times while cooking.
6. You can tell the shrimp are done when they are opaque and pink.
7. Sprinkle with paprika when serving.

TIP
To defrost shrimp, just run them under cold water in a colander or strainer for several minutes just before cooking them. Defrosted shrimp only last for two days.

TIP
Write the date you purchased a spice on the jar. Most spices lose their potency after 6 months to 1 year.

Microwave

Paper towels

Glass casserole

Gretchen G's Grillin' Mango Shrimp Kabobs

12 frozen, defrosted, shelled and deveined shrimp
1 green pepper cut in 1 inch squares
1 onion cut in 1 inch squares
1 ripe mango cut in 1 inch squares
1 lime cut into wedges
1/2 teaspoon salt
1/8 teaspoon black pepper
canola cooking spray

1. Sprinkle the shrimp with salt and pepper.
2. Put on 1 shrimp, 1 pepper, 1 onion and 1 mango cube onto each skewer.
3. Spray a grill rack with cooking spray.
4. Heat the grill to medium high heat.
5. Grill each skewer about 2 minutes each side.
6. Squeeze lime juice on the kabobs.

TIP

To dice a mango slice off one of the wide sides of the unpeeled fruit cutting as close to the seed as possible. Repeat with the other wide side, then slice off the remaining narrow pieces. Take one of the large pieces in your hand and using a sharp paring knife, score the fruit into 1 inch cubes not cutting through the skin. Turn the piece upside down and pop the pieces out away from the skin.

Grill

Skewers

Kay G's Saucy Shrimp In Red Wine Sauce

1/8 cup butter or margarine
1 small yellow onion, chopped in 1/2 inch pieces
1 teaspoon fresh minced garlic
1 small can tomato sauce (8 ounces)
1/2 cup red wine
1/8 cup all purpose flour
1/4 teaspoon italian seasoning
1/2 pound frozen shrimp, defrosted, shelled and deveined

1. Combine the onion and garlic in a medium microwaveable dish.
2. Microwave on High for about 4 minutes until the onion is tender.
3. Stir in remaining ingredients except for the shrimp.
4. Cover the dish with a paper towel and microwave on Medium High for 5 minutes.
5. Add the shrimp to wine sauce and microwave on High for about 3 minutes until shrimp turns pink.

TIP
Do not over cook the shrimp or they will become tough.

TIP
No italian seasoning? Use 1 part garlic powder, 2 parts oregano and 2 parts dried basil.

TIP
Fresh herbs can be frozen in plastic bags or ice cube trays so they are always readily available.

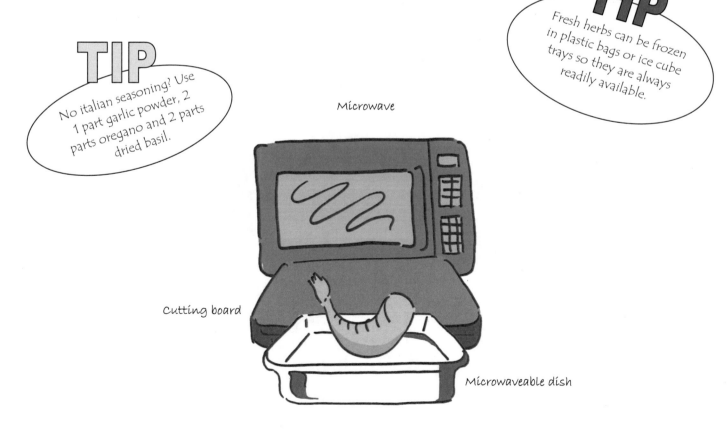

Microwave

Cutting board

Microwaveable dish

Wendy B's Healthy Baked Eggplant Parmesan

1 small eggplant sliced in 1/2 inch thick
1 tablespoon olive oil
1/2 cup skim milk
2 tablespoons all purpose flour
1 teaspoon fresh minced garlic
1/2 cup pasta sauce
1/2 cup part-skim mozzarella cheese
1/2 cup grated parmesan cheese
salt and pepper

TIP
Use a serrated knife to cut eggplant for easier slicing.

Preheat oven to 450°

1. Arrange sliced eggplant on a rimmed cookie sheet.
2. Brush the eggplant on both sides with olive oil and season with salt and pepper.
3. Bake until golden brown for about 20 minutes turning slices halfway through the baking.
4. In a small saucepan mix milk, flour, garlic and pasta sauce. Bring to a boil on medium heat, then reduce to a simmer on low heat and cook until thickened 2 or 3 minutes.
5. Spread 1/4 cup pasta sauce on bottom of small baking pan.
6. Alternate layers of eggplant, sauce and top with cheese.
7. Bake until brown and bubbling for about 10 to 15 minutes.

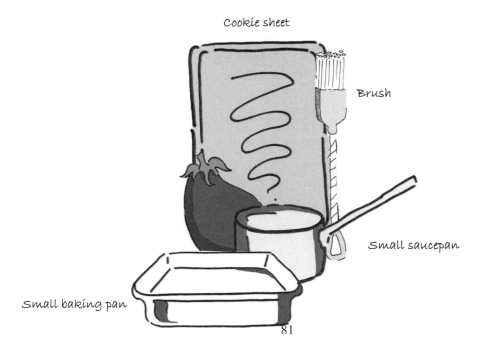

Cookie sheet

Brush

Small saucepan

Small baking pan

Sophie L's Loaded Grilled Cheese Sandwiches

4 slices of white, whole wheat or multi-grain bread
4 slices of your favorite cheese
1 tablespoon softened butter or margarine

1. Heat a grill pan or small skillet over medium low heat.
2. Spread one side generously with 1/2 the butter and place the butter side down in the skillet.
3. Place two slices of cheese on top of the bread in the skillet.
4. Use the remaining butter to butter one side of the other slice of bread.
5. Place it on top of the cheese with the butter side facing up.
6. Cook the sandwich until the bottom slice is lightly browned (you can use a spatula or kitchen tong to gently lift the sandwich up slightly to watch if it is browning).
7. Once it is browned, flip it over and cook the other side until it is browned and the cheese is melted.
8. Repeat with the remaining two slices of bread.

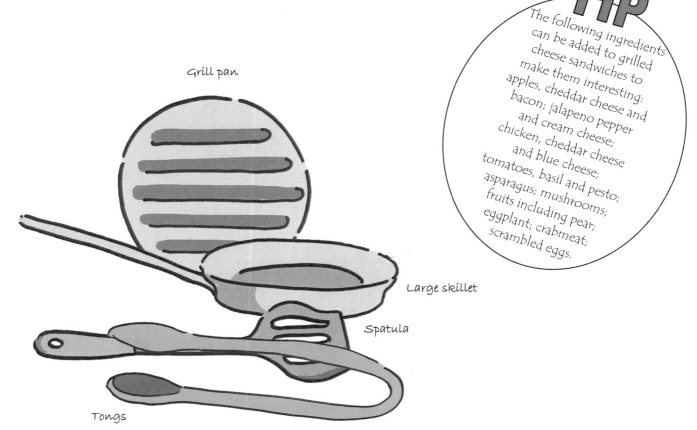

Grill pan

Large skillet

Spatula

Tongs

TIP

The following ingredients can be added to grilled cheese sandwiches to make them interesting: apples, cheddar cheese and bacon; jalapeno pepper and cream cheese; chicken, cheddar cheese and blue cheese; tomatoes, basil and pesto; asparagus; mushrooms; fruits including pear; eggplant; crabmeat; scrambled eggs.

Jamie K's Microwave Mac And Cheese

6 tablespoons butter or margarine
2 tablespoons all purpose flour
1/2 teaspoon dry mustard powder
1 1/2 cups milk
2 cups shredded cheddar cheese
8 ounces elbow macaroni
1/2 cup seasoned breadcrumbs

TIP

Always give your flour bag or canister a shake to aerate the flour for more accurate measuring.

1. Cook the macaroni following package directions in a medium saucepan.
2. Drain the macaroni and set aside.
3. Place 3 tablespoons margarine or butter in a large microwaveable dish and cook on High until melted (about 30 seconds to 1 minute.
4. In the microwaveable dish, blend the flour, mustard, and milk. Stir.
5. Microwave on High for 6 minutes until thickened.
6. Stir in the cheese and microwave on High to soften cheese for about 1 minute.
7. Add cooked macaroni to the dish.
8. Place 3 remaining tablespoons of butter or margarine in a small bowl. Microwave on High until melted (about 30 seconds).
9. Mix the breadcrumbs in the melted butter or margarine and sprinkle over the macaroni casserole.
10. Microwave on Medium High until heated through (about 5-7 minutes).

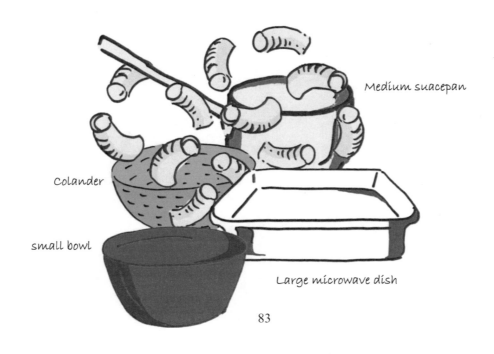

Medium suacepan

Colander

small bowl

Large microwave dish

entrements

relishes

Side dishes

accompaniments

veggies

pastas

Adrienne H's Honey Glazed Sweet Potatoes

3 sweet potatoes or yams
1/8 cup olive oil
honey

Preheat oven to 400°

1. Peel the sweet potatoes and cut them into quarters lengthwise.
2. Rinse the potatoes in cold water and pat dry.
3. Place the potatoes in a large bowl, add the olive oil and toss to coat.
4. Arrange them on a rimmed cookie sheet in a single layer without overlapping and bake for 45 minutes.
5. Remove from the oven and brush with honey.
6. Bake for another 15 minutes until tender and slightly brown.

TIP

Sweet potatoes come in yellow and orange varieties. Either one can be used for this recipe.

Cookie sheet

Large bowl

Cooking brush

Potato peeler

Maxine B's Better Sweet Potato Fries

2 large sweet potatoes, peeled and cut into wedges
1/2 teaspoon salt
1/4 teaspoon black pepper
canola cooking spray

Preheat oven to 400°

TIP

If you don't have cooking spray use a basting brush with canola or olive oil to coat the cookie sheet. Put the sweet potato wedges in a bowl with a small amount of oil and toss them around. Then follow steps 4-5.

1. Coat a large rimmed cookie sheet well with cooking spray.
2. Arrange the potato wedges on the prepared cookie sheet (do not overlap pieces).
3. Coat the potatoes generously with cooking spray.
4. Lightly sprinkle the potatoes with salt and black pepper.
5. Bake uncovered for 30 minutes, until tender and golden brown.

TIP

You can sprinkle potatoes with white or brown sugar, paprika, garlic powder, ginger, pumpkin spice or any other spices you have on hand to create different flavors.

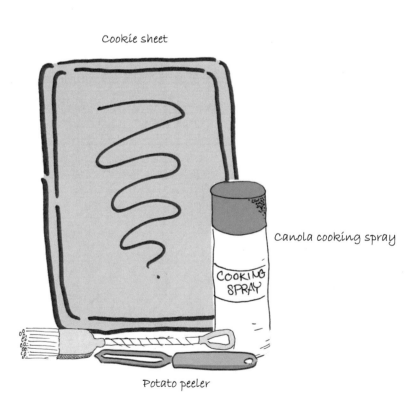

Cookie sheet

Canola cooking spray

COOKING SPRAY

Basting brush

Potato peeler

Joan S's Sweet Potato Puree

2 medium sweet potatoes
2 medium white potatoes
4 tablespoons milk
1 stick unsalted butter or margarine
1/3 cup brown sugar

1. Peel the potatoes and cut into 1 inch cubes.
2. Place the potatoes in a medium saucepan, cover with water and bring to a boil on high heat.
3. Reduce heat after the water has boiled to medium.
4. Cook for 20 more minutes or until the potatoes are tender.
5. Drain the potatoes, return to saucepan and cook for 3-5 minutes on low heat to remove any moisture.
6. Turn off heat and add the remaining ingredients.
7. Mash the potatoes with a potato masher or hand-held immersion blender until smooth.

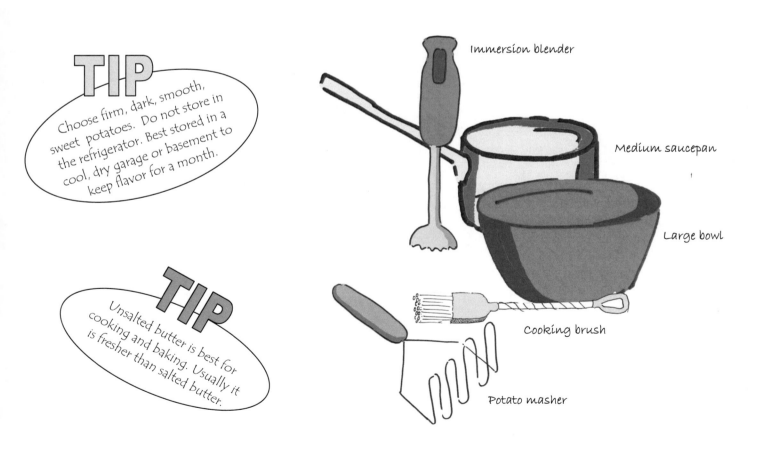

TIP Choose firm, dark, smooth, sweet potatoes. Do not store in the refrigerator. Best stored in a cool, dry garage or basement to keep flavor for a month.

TIP Unsalted butter is best for cooking and baking. Usually it is fresher than salted butter.

Immersion blender

Medium saucepan

Large bowl

Cooking brush

Potato masher

Susie R's Cheese And Chive Potatoes

1 pound yukon potatoes
1/2 cup shredded cheddar cheese
1/2 cup alfredo sauce
1/4 cup chopped chives (optional)
1/4 cup milk
canola cooking spray

TIP
Chives are available either fresh or freeze-dried.

Heat oven to 350°

1. Coat a large baking pan with cooking spray.
2. Slice the potatoes into thin slices about 1/4 inch thick.
3. Mix the potatoes with 1/4 cup cheese and all the other ingredients.
4. Spoon into the prepared pan, cover with foil and bake for about 45 minutes to 1 hour.
5. Remove foil from baking dish, sprinkle with remaining 1/4 cup cheese and bake for another 20-30 minutes.
6. You can tell the dish is ready when the potatoes are soft when pierced with a fork and mixture is bubbly.

TIP
When cooking unpeeled potatoes, a grapefruit serrated knife works well to remove the eyes and the serrated edge cleans off the dirt without removing the peel.

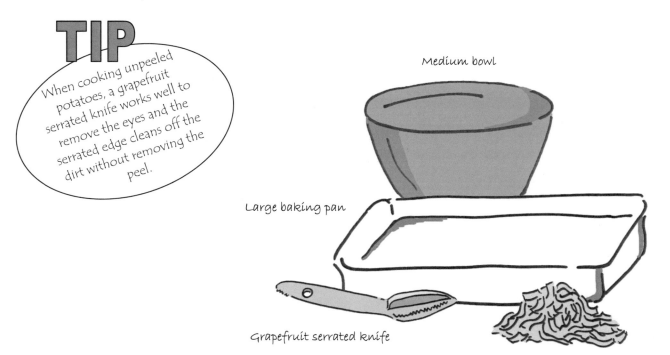

Medium bowl

Large baking pan

Grapefruit serrated knife

Meredith B's Microwave Potatoes

2 large potatoes, such as idaho
2 tablespoons extra virgin olive oil
2 tablespoons butter or margarine
1 small onion, peeled and halved
1 tablespoon grill seasoning

TIP
Serve with scrambled eggs for a scrumptious brunch.

1. Wash, scrub and pierce the potatoes with a fork. Wrap them in a paper towel.
2. Cook the potatoes in a microwave oven about 6 minutes on High.
3. Let them stand for 5 minutes then coarsely mash the potatoes with a hand-held immersion blender.
4. Heat the extra virgin olive oil and butter in a nonstick medium skillet on medium high heat for 3 minutes.
5. Add the potatoes to the skillet.
6. Grate the onions over the skillet with a hand held grater .
7. Toss the potatoes and onions to coat evenly in butter and oil and season with grill seasoning.
8. Continue cooking the potato mixture for 6-8 minutes until brown and crisp.

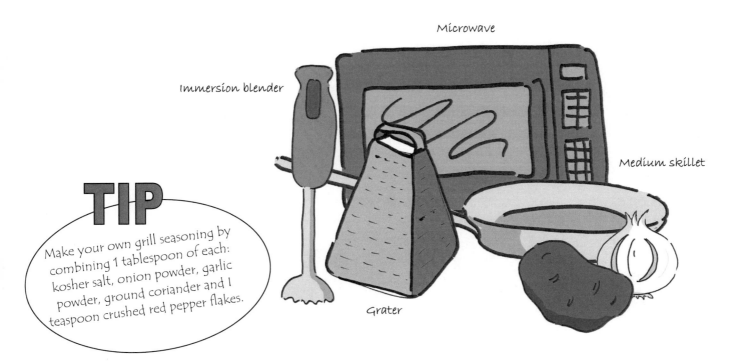

TIP
Make your own grill seasoning by combining 1 tablespoon of each: kosher salt, onion powder, garlic powder, ground coriander and 1 teaspoon crushed red pepper flakes.

Immersion blender

Microwave

Medium skillet

Grater

Marsha B's Beer Muffins

4 cups buttermilk baking mix
1 can beer (12 ounces)
2 tablespoons sugar
canola cooking spray

Preheat oven to 400°

1. Spray 2 muffin tins with cooking spray.
2. Mix all the ingredients in a large bowl to make batter.
3. Pour the batter into the prepared pans.
4. Bake 15 to 20 minutes until golden brown.

TIP
Add raisins or shredded cheese for a variety.

TIP
If your muffin tins are oversized and you do not have enough batter to fill all the muffin cups, fill the empty ones with water. This will prevent the muffins you are baking from drying out.

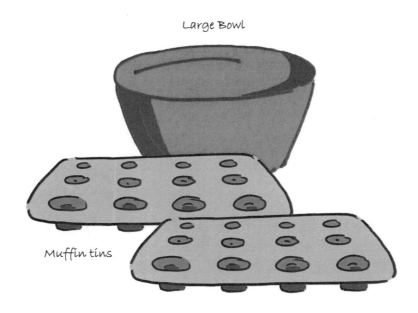

Large Bowl

Muffin tins

Karen F's Fresh Strawberry Basil Salad

1 1/2 tablespoons olive oil
1 1/2 tablespoons balsamic vinegar
2 cups romaine lettuce (about 1/2 head)
1 cup fresh strawberries
1/2 vidalia onion
1/8 cup fresh basil
salt and black pepper

1. Wash the romaine lettuce and let it dry thoroughly.
2. Combine the olive oil, balsamic vinegar and a dash of salt and black pepper in a large bowl to make the dressing. Mix well.
3. Slice the onion and strawberries into thin slices about 1/8 inch thick.
4. Gently tear off basil leaves from the stem of the plant.
5. Combine the lettuce, strawberries, onion and basil.
6. Pour the dressing over the lettuce mixture and toss gently to coat well.

TIP
You can use a plastic straw to remove the hull of a strawberry, just push it through from the top of the berry.

TIP
Always wash your strawberries right before using them. Keeping them dry helps them stay fresh. If there are any spoiled ones in the batch get rid of them right away as 1 rotten berry can spoil the rest.

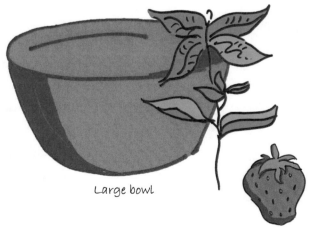

Large bowl

Renee D's Romaine Lettuce With Parmesan Ribbons

1/3 cup extra virgin olive oil
2 tablespoons balsamic vinegar
1 tablespoon red wine vinegar
1 1/2 teaspoons brown sugar
1/4 teaspoon salt
1/4 teaspoon pepper
1 small red onion sliced in 1/2 inch slices
1 package romaine lettuce hearts
1/4 pound block of parmesan cheese

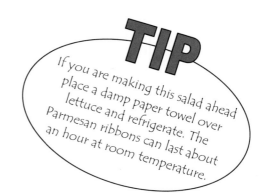

TIP

If you are making this salad ahead place a damp paper towel over lettuce and refrigerate. The Parmesan ribbons can last about an hour at room temperature.

1. Wash, trim and tear the lettuce into individual leaves and dry them. Set aside.
2. Combine the oil, vinegars, sugar, salt and pepper in a small microwaveable bowl to make the dressing. Stir well until combined.
3. Add the onion, cover with plastic wrap and microwave the dressing on High for 2 minutes.
4. Remove the onions from the dressing and set aside on a plate.
5. To serve, arrange the lettuce leaves on a serving dish, sprinkle the cooked onions over the lettuce. Mix the dressing and pour enough to just moisten the lettuce.
6. Use a vegetable peeler to make long strands of parmesan cheese and place them on top of the salad.

TIP

You can add walnuts or dried cranberries to give the salad some crunch and refrigerate the leftover dressing.

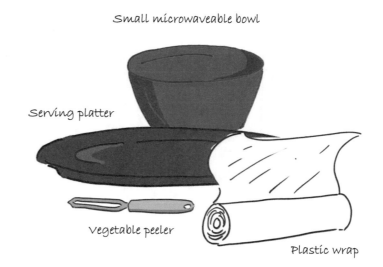

Small microwaveable bowl

Serving platter

Vegetable peeler

Plastic wrap

Faye R's Really Good Orzo Salad

1 cup orzo
salt and pepper
1 tablespoon plus 1 teaspoon olive oil
2 medium zucchini, quartered lengthwise and thinly sliced
1/2 teaspoon fresh minced garlic
1/2 cup fresh basil leaves, torn
1-2 tablespoon white wine vinegar

TIP

If storing, cover and refrigerate 1 day, bring to room temperature before serving.

1. In a medium pot of boiling salted water, cook orzo until al dente, according to package instructions.
2. Drain well using a colander or slotted spoon.
3. Spread on a rimmed baking sheet to cool completely.
4. In a large skillet, heat 1 tablespoon oil over medium heat.
5. Add the zucchini and garlic, to the skillet and season with salt and pepper.
6. Cook, tossing occasionally until crisp tender, 4-5 minutes.
7. Transfer the orzo to a medium bowl, add the zucchini mixture, basil, vinegar and remaining teaspoon oil.
8. Toss to combine.

TIP

Orzo is a form of macaroni shaped like a large grain of rice.

Cookie sheet

Colander

Medium bowl

Large skillet

Slotted spoon

Alexis C's Cranberry Coleslaw

1/8 cup mayonnaise
1 tablespoon sugar
1/2 tablespoon white vinegar
1/8 cup dried cranberries (found with the nuts and other dried fruits)
2 cups green or savoy shredded cabbage (1/2 small head or buy pre-shredded)

1. Place the cabbage in a medium bowl and set aside.
2. Make the dressing by mixing the mayonnaise, sugar and vinegar in a small bowl.
3. Stir the cranberries into the dressing.
4. Pour the dressing over the cabbage and stir to coat well.
5. Cover the bowl with plastic wrap and refrigerate for 45 minutes to 4 hours before serving.

TIP You can substitute fresh cranberries for the dried cranberries in the fall, when they are in season.

TIP Soak cabbage in cold water with a 1/2 tablespoon of salt dissolved in it for about 10 minutes to keep it crisp before shredding it. Just rinse it well and dry it with paper towels, then slice with a large sharp knife.

Medium bowl

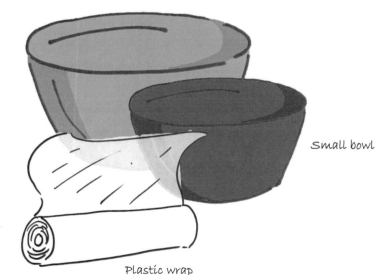

Small bowl

Plastic wrap

Hillary Y's You'll Love It Asian Slaw

2 packages asian noodle soup mix
1 bag pre-packages coleslaw mix (found in the produce aisle)
1 cup sunflower seeds
1 cup sliced almonds
1/2 cup sugar
3/4 cup canola oil
1/2 cup white vinegar

TIP
If you keep vinegar in the refrigerator it will stay fresh longer.

1. Remove the seasoning packet from the soup mix and set aside.
2. Break the noodles up and put in the bottom of a large bowl.
3. Add 1/2 of the coleslaw, 1/2 of the sunflower seeds, 1/2 of the almonds to the bowl.
4. Repeat the above.
5. In a small bowl mix the vinegar, sugar, oil and seasoning from the package of soup.
6. Pour on top of the noodle coleslaw mixture.
7. Refrigerate for a few hours before serving.

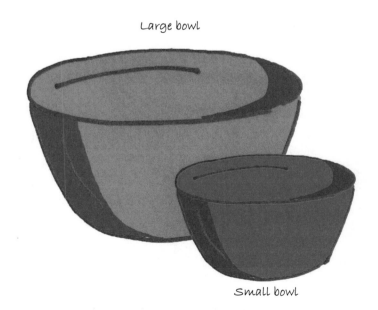

Large bowl

Small bowl

Fran L's Frozen Gnocchi With Zucchini

1 tablespoon olive oil
1 large zucchini
2 tablespoons fresh minced garlic
1 package grape tomatoes
1 package frozen gnocchi (15-16 ounces)
2 tablespoons parmesan grated cheese
1 tablespoon butter or margarine

TIP

Frozen zucchini (also known as green squash) can be substituted for fresh.

1. Cut the tomatoes in half.
2. In a large skillet heat oil over medium high heat.
3. Cut the zucchini into 1 inch slices and add, along with garlic, to the skillet.
4. Cook stirring occasionally until the zucchini is tender about 4-5 minutes.
5. Add the tomatoes to the skillet and cook stirring for about 2 minutes.
6. Meanwhile boil water in a large saucepan.
7. When the water boils, add gnocchi and cook until they are soft.
8. Reserve 1/2 cup of water that gnocchi was boiled in and drain the gnocchi.
9. Transfer the cooked gnocchi to the skillet.
10. Add the gnocchi to the skillet and add enough water that you saved to make a sauce.
11. Remove from heat, add the cheese and butter.
12. Serve when the cheese and butter are melted.

Medium saucepan

Colander

Medium skillet

Dale C's Company Fried Ravioli

TIP
This is a bit more challenging, but worth the work! Serve it as an hors d'oeuvre or as a side dish.

1 package frozen 4-cheese ravioli
3/4 cup grated Parmesan
1/4 cup milk
1 egg beaten
1/4 tsp salt
1/8 tsp ground black pepper
oil
jar of spaghetti sauce

1. Boil the water in large saucepan, cook the ravioli for 2 minutes.
2. Place cooked ravioli on paper towels to drain, set aside.
3. Pour the cheese into shallow bowl.
4. Mix the milk, egg, salt and pepper in a bowl.
5. Dip the ravioli in the egg mixture then dredge them in the cheese.
6. Pour the oil to a depth of 1/2 inch in a skillet.
7. Fry the ravioli, in batches, 2 minutes on each side, or until golden.
8. Drain on paper towels.
9. Heat the sauce in the microwave or in a small saucepan.
10. Serve with sauce on side.

Large saucepan

Large skillet

Small bowls

Annie W's Risotto With Cheddar Cheese

2 tablespoons butter or margarine
1/4 cup onion diced in 1/4 inch pieces
1/2 cup arborio rice
1/4 cup hot water
1 chicken bouillon cube
1/8 teaspoon nutmeg powder
1/2 cup shredded cheddar cheese

1. In a medium saucepan melt butter over medium high heat. Cook until the butter starts to brown, about 3 minutes.
2. Stir in the onions and rice, and cook for 2 minutes stirring frequently.
3. Add the hot water, bouillon cube and nutmeg. Increase heat to high and bring to a boil stirring occasionally.
4. Cover the saucepan and reduce heat to low. Simmer for about 10 minutes.
5. Remove the pan from heat and add cheddar cheese.

TIP
Chicken bouillon can be found in the soup aisle. It comes in small packets or cubes.

TIP
Cooking times for risotto vary. Rice should be somewhat firm but creamy when finished. It will continue to cook and absorb liquid as it sits.

Medium saucepan

Bonnie K. M's Kreamy Korn Souffle

1 small can creamed corn
1 small can whole kernel corn
1/2 stick butter or margarine
8 ounces sour cream
1 box corn muffin mix (8 ounces)
1 egg, beaten

TIP

If you double the recipe, an alternate way to make this is to use 3 cans of creamed corn and 1 can of whole kernel corn resulting in a creamier cornbread.

Preheat oven to 350°

1. Melt the butter in a small bowl in the microwave for about 1 minute. Let it cool.
2. Put all the other ingredients in a large bowl (including the liquid from the corn).
3. Add the butter to the corn muffin mixture.
4. Pour the batter into a medium baking pan (it will be lumpy).
5. Bake for about 45 minutes or until the top is brown and a toothpick comes out clean.

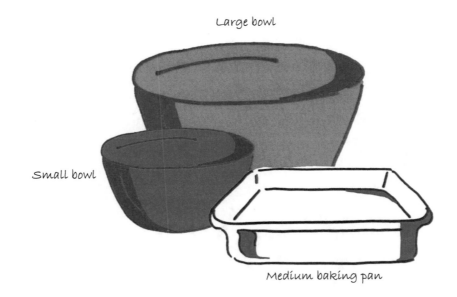

Large bowl

Small bowl

Medium baking pan

Pamela S's Sesame Peanut Spaghetti

2 cups cold cooked spaghetti
3 tablespoons smooth peanut butter
2 tablespoons soy sauce
2 tablespoons rice vinegar
2 tablespoons water
1 tablespoon orange juice
2 teaspoons sesame oil

1. Mix all the ingredients in a large bowl.
2. Add broccoli, cooked chicken, snow peas, sliced peppers, water chestnuts or a combination as desired.

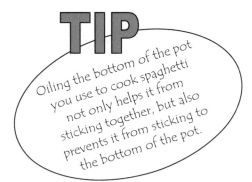

TIP

Oiling the bottom of the pot you use to cook spaghetti not only helps it from sticking together, but also prevents it from sticking to the bottom of the pot.

TIP

Never rinse spaghetti after it is cooked. Rinsing pasta removes starch from the surface preventing any sauce from sticking to the pasta and making it tastier.

Large bowl

Heidi A's Au Gratin Cauliflower

1 small head of fresh cauliflower
1 tablespoon water
1/2 tablespoon butter or margarine
1/2 tablespoon all purpose flour
1/4 cup milk
1/2 teaspoon mustard
1/2 cup cheddar cheese
hungarian paprika

TIP
You can substitute broccoli if you don't like cauliflower.

1. Break off florets of cauliflower and cover them with water in a medium microwaveable dish with a top.
2. Cover and microwave on High for about 4 minutes or until tender.
3. Drain the cauliflower and set aside.
4. Put butter or margarine in a small microwaveable bowl and microwave on High for about 30 seconds until melted.
5. Blend in the milk, mustard and salt to make a sauce.
6. Microwave the sauce at Medium High for about 2 minutes until thickened (stir a few times while cooking).
7. Stir in cheese until melted.
8. Pour the sauce over the cauliflower and sprinkle with paprika.

TIP
After cutting off the top florets of the cauliflower, use a melon baller to make it easier to remove the florets closer to the top.

Microwave

Small bowl

Medium microwave dish with top

Sue E's Garlic Green Beans

1 small box frozen green beans
1/2 teaspoon fresh minced garlic
1 tablespoon butter or margarine

1. Cut the butter up into small pieces.
2. Put all the ingredients in a small microwaveable dish.
3. Cover the microwaveable dish with a paper towel.
4. Microwave on High for about 5 minutes or until the beans are crisp.
5. Stir and strain with a slotted spoon.

TIP

Covering a dish with a paper towel helps keep your microwave clean.

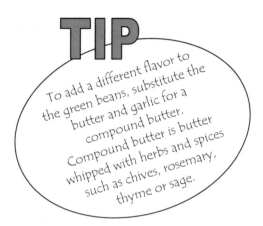

TIP

To add a different flavor to the green beans, substitute the butter and garlic for a compound butter. Compound butter is butter whipped with herbs and spices such as chives, rosemary, thyme or sage.

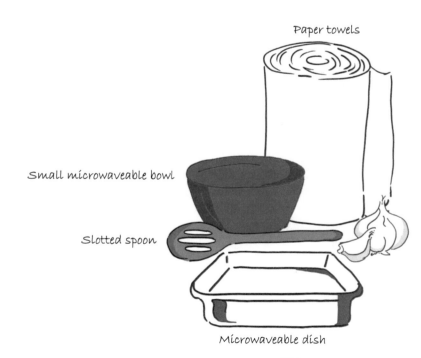

Paper towels

Small microwaveable bowl

Slotted spoon

Microwaveable dish

Stacia C's Made In The Microwave Beans

1 pound fresh green beans, stem ends removed
1/2 teaspoon fresh minced garlic
1 tablespoon butter or margarine
salt

1. Place the beans, garlic, butter and 1/4 cup water in a medium microwaveable dish with a lid.
2. Season with salt.
3. Cover and microwave on High until beans are crisp, 6-7 minutes. Stir, and pour off any excess liquid.

TIP

Add other fresh vegetables like corn, peas or carrots to make a vegetable medley. Cooking time may vary.

TIP

You can substitute frozen green beans if you want to.

Microwave

Microwaveable dish

Tilly R's Caramelized Tomatoes

2 large ripe tomatoes cut in half horizontally
2 teaspoons extra virgin olive oil
1/4 teaspoon fresh minced garlic
1/2 tablespoon chopped fresh basil
Salt and pepper

TIP
Serve these hot or at room temperature.

Heat oven to 325°

1. Place the tomatoes on a cookie sheet cut sides up.
2. Drizzle with the oil and sprinkle with a little salt and pepper.
3. Bake for 1-2 hours until the tomatoes caramelize (see tip).
4. Spread the tomatoes with garlic and basil just before serving.

TIP
Caramelizing is another term for browning. Typically onions are caramelized for a topping on burgers or steaks.

Cookie sheet

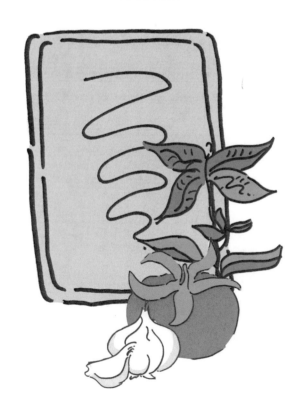

Brenda K's Very Veggie Stew

2 yellow onions
1/2 pound baby carrots
2 red peppers
2 beefsteak or plum tomatoes
2 ribs celery
1 zucchini
1/2 pound fresh green beans
1 cup tomato paste
1 tablespoon sugar
1 carton of vegetable broth (32 ounces)

1. Slice all the vegetables into medium size pieces (about 2 inches).
2. Pour the vegetable broth in a large saucepan.
3. Place the vegetables except for the tomatoes in the saucepan and heat on medium high heat for 10 minutes.
4. Add the tomato paste, sugar and tomatoes.
5. Cover and cook until the vegetables are soft (about 20 minutes).

TIP
To pick fresh tomatoes, look for ones that are completely free of blemishes and soft spots.

TIP
To pick the freshest zucchini, look for firm, heavy squash that have a moist stem and shiny skin.

Cutting board

Large saucepan

Geri N's Nicely Roasted Parmesan Asparagus

1 pound fresh asparagus
1 tablespoon olive oil
salt and black pepper
1/4 cup grated parmesan cheese

TIP
Make sure the asparagus are spread out in a single layer and not overlapping so they will roast properly in the oven.

Preheat oven to 400°

1. Rinse the asparagus under cool water to remove any grit. Snap off the bottom with your fingers (the stems will break naturally).
2. Dry the spears by rolling them between two towels.
3. Cut the spears into 2 inch pieces and place them in a medium baking pan.
4. Sprinkle the asparagus with olive oil, then lightly sprinkle them with salt and black pepper. Move them around in the pan to make sure they are evenly coated.
5. Bake uncovered in oven for about 10-15 minutes until the asparagus is crisp and tender (this is actually called roasting vegetables if you see that in another cookbook).
6. Place the spears on a serving platter and sprinkle with the cheese.

TIP
Other vegetables can be substituted for the asparagus like broccoli, cauliflower, eggplant or zucchini.

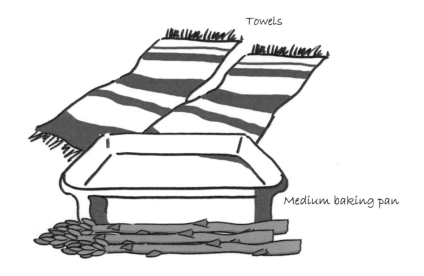

Towels

Medium baking pan

Andi L's Asparagus And Tomatoes With Balsamic Vinegar

1/2 pound fresh asparagus
1 teaspoon olive oil
1 cup grape tomatoes sliced in half
1/4 teaspoon fresh minced garlic
1 tablespoon balsamic vinegar
3 tablespoons goat cheese

TIP

Bend the asparagus close to the bottom. They will naturally break at the most tender point.

1. Wash the asparagus gently and break off ends (see tip).
2. Fill a large saucepan with water and bring it to a boil over medium high heat.
3. Cook the asparagus in the boiling water until crisp and tender (about 3 minutes).
4. Drain and remove the asparagus from the saucepan and set aside.
5. Heat the olive oil in a medium skillet over medium high heat.
6. Add the tomatoes, garlic and asparagus to the skillet and continue cooking for about 5 minutes.
7. Stir in the vinegar and cook for another 3 or 4 minutes.
8. Arrange the asparagus and tomatoes on a platter and sprinkle with goat cheese.

Large saucepan

Medium skillet

cake

afters

confections

FLOUR

sweets

desserts

pastries

Susan M's Best Baked Apples

1 macintosh apple
1 teaspoon brown sugar for each apple
1/8 teaspoon cinnamon for each apple
ice cream or whipped cream for topping

1. Wash and core an apple for each guest you wish to serve.
2. Put each apple in a microwaveable dish.
3. Fill the center hole with the brown sugar and cinnamon.
4. Microwave each apple for 3 minutes on High or until soft.
5. Serve warm with ice cream or whipped cream.

TIP

Raisins can be added to these apples for a variety.

TIP

Other kinds of apples that are ideal for baking are Golden Delicious, Honeycrisp or Empire.

Microwave

Knife   Microwaveable dish

D.J. W's Waterbath Cheesecakes

2 large eggs
3/4 teaspoon pure vanilla extract
1/2 cup sugar
3/4 pound of ricotta cheese
1 1/2 teaspoons all purpose flour
canola cooking spray
jar of raspberry or strawberry pie filling (found in the baking aisle) or
fresh fruit and berries

TIP
Cooking the cheesecakes in a water bath helps them from cracking on top.

Preheat oven to 350°

1. Line two muffin pans with foil muffin pan liners.
2. Lightly spray them with cooking spray.
3. Using an electric mixer beat the eggs and vanilla on high until fluffy for around 6 minutes in a large mixing bowl. Slowly beat in the sugar.
4. On low speed mix in the cheese and flour. Fill the muffin tins 1/2 full with the batter.
5. Carefully place the filled muffin tins in a large roasting pan and fill the pan with about 2 -4 cups of water to make a water bath.
6. Bake for about 20 minutes or until center of the cheesecakes set (you can tell by inserting a toothpick, it should come out clean).
7. Remove the muffin tins from the oven and let the cheesecakes cool.
8. Top them with the raspberry or strawberry pie filling. You can also top with whipped cream if you wish.

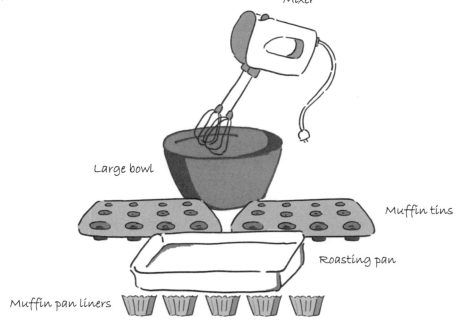

Mixer

Large bowl

Muffin tins

Roasting pan

Muffin pan liners

Jessica M's Mama Do I Love It Cheesecake

3 pounds ricotta cheese
9 large eggs
1 1/2 cup sugar
1/4 cup heavy cream
2 tablespoons vanilla extract

Preheat oven to 350°

1. Butter and flour a 10 inch springform pan and place it on a cookie sheet.
2. Combine all the ingredients in a large bowl and mix using an electric mixer till well blended.
3. Pour into the prepared springform pan and bake for 1 1/2 hours.
4. Turn off the oven and let the pan rest inside the oven for an additional 30 minutes.

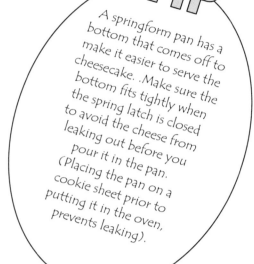

TIP

A springform pan has a bottom that comes off to make it easier to serve the cheesecake. .Make sure the bottom fits tightly when the spring latch is closed to avoid the cheese from leaking out before you pour it in the pan. (Placing the pan on a cookie sheet prior to putting it in the oven, prevents leaking).

Cookie sheet

Mixer

Large bowl

Springform pan

TIP

To butter and flour a pan, use a paper towel and a 1 inch piece of bar butter to apply a thin, even layer to the bottom and sides of the springform pan. Add about 2 tablespoons of all purpose flour and gently tilt the pan side to side to cover the bottom and sides with the flour. If you need to add more flour for the sides just invert the pan after all sides are coated and make sure to you remove any excess to avoid a flour taste to the cake.

Mickey C's Chewy Chocolate Chip Cookies

2 sticks unsalted butter or margarine
3/4 cup light brown sugar
1/4 cup sugar
1 teaspoon vanilla extract
1 large egg, beaten
1/2 teaspoon baking soda
2 cups all purpose flour
1 package chocolate chips (12 ounces)

TIP

For thick and chewy cookies use butter and eggs right out of the refrigerator (dough will be chilled more). For thin and crispy cookies, let the butter and egg come to room temperature.

Preheat oven to 375°

1. Beat the butter, brown sugar and white sugar with an electric mixer or spoon until well blended.
2. Add the vanilla, beaten egg and baking soda.
3. Add the flour and mix until well blended using a wooden spoon.
4. Stir in the chocolate chips also using a wooden spoon.
5. Spoon the mixture on an ungreased cookie sheet about 2 inches apart.
6. Bake until golden brown about 10 minutes.
7. Remove the cookies to a wire rack and cool.

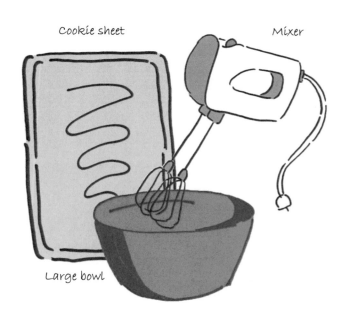

Cookie sheet

Mixer

Large bowl

Eve F's Everyone Loves Easy Chocolate Cookies

1 cup semisweet chocolate chips
1 cup brown sugar
1/3 cup canola oil
2 large eggs
1 teaspoon vanilla
1 cup all purpose flour
1 teaspoon baking powder
1/4 teaspoon salt
1/2 cup chopped walnuts
1/4 cup confectioners sugar (found in the baking aisle)
canola cooking spray

TIP
Eggs come in different sizes, in non-baking recipes all sizes are interchangeable.

TIP
When baking you always mix the "dry" ingredients flour, salt, baking powder, etc.) separately from the "wet" ingredients (eggs, oil, sugar) so that the ingredients mix properly and the dough is the right consistency.

Preheat oven to 350°

1. Place the chocolate chips in a medium microwaveable bowl.
2. Microwave on High for about 2 minutes until melted.
3. Using an electric mixer mix in the brown sugar and oil.
4. Add eggs one at a time beating well after each egg. Stir in the vanilla.
5. Mix the flour, baking powder and salt in a large bowl.
6. Stir in the chocolate mixture and nuts.
7. Place the bowl of dough in the refrigerator for at least 1 hour to chill.
8. Spray a cookie sheet with cooking spray.
9. Pour the confectioners sugar into a plate.
10. Make 1 inch balls of dough and roll them in the sugar until they are well coated.
11. Place them on the prepared cookie sheet and bake 10-12 minutes.

Cookie sheet

Mixer

Canola cooking spray

Large bowl

Plate

Medium bowl

Melissa F's Devilish Dirt Cake

1 box of sandwich cookies (16 ounces)
1 cup powdered sugar (also called confectioners sugar)
1 package cream cheese (8 ounces)
1/4 cup softened butter or margarine
2 packages vanilla instant pudding (3.9 ounces each package)
3 1/2 cups milk
12 ounces frozen whipped topping

1. Crush up the sandwich cookies and set them aside in a small bowl.
2. Mix the powdered sugar, cream cheese and margarine together in a medium bowl.
3. Mix the pudding and milk in a 3rd bowl and let it stand for 10 minutes to thicken.
4. Fold the frozen whipped topping into the pudding mixture then fold in the cream cheese mixture (see tip).
5. Layer the crushed sandwich cookies and pudding mixture in a sand bucket or clean clay pot ending with crushed cookies. Garnish with the gummy worms.

TIP

To fold in ingredients use a spatula or a spoon and gently use a downward motion on one side of the bowl across the bottom to the opposite side. Rotate the bowl and repeat this motion. You will notice a marbleized effect, as opposed to all the ingredients being mixed totally together.

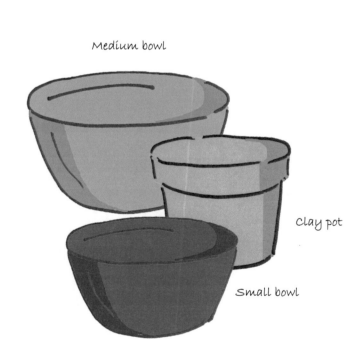

Medium bowl

Clay pot

Small bowl

Linda S's Easy Dump Cake

1 can apple pie filling
1 can pineapple, crushed (in its own juice which you use)
1/2 bag yellow cake mix
1 small can walnuts, chopped
1 package coconut flakes
1/2 pound melted butter or margarine
1 container frozen whipped topping

Preheat oven to 350°

1. Layer in a 9 x 12 pan all the ingredients (except the frozen whipped topping) in the above order.
2. Bake for 40 minutes.
3. Top each serving with frozen whipped topping.

TIP

Experiment using other flavors than apple pie filling (strawberry, blueberry, etc.) and other fruits (peaches, cherries, etc.).

TIP

To impress a date and set a nice table you should have a pretty centerpiece. An easy and inexpensive one, is to wrap aluminum foil around the ends of asparagus, anchor them in a small vase filled with shelled pistachio nuts.

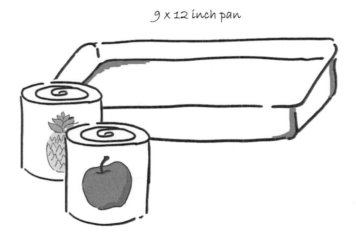

9 x 12 inch pan

Luda G's Lemon Pudding Cake

1 package yellow cake mix
1 package lemon gelatin mix
3/4 cups canola oil
3/4 cups of water or orange juice
4 large eggs (beaten separately)

Preheat oven to 350°

TIP

No tube pan,? Use a bundt pan instead. Always check the cake is done by inserting a toothpick in the middle. If it comes out clean, the cake is done.

1. Combine the lemon gelatin mix with the cake mix in a medium bowl. Mix using an electric mixer on slow speed.
2. Add the water or orange juice and oil to the bowl and mix.
3. Beat the eggs (one at a time) in a small bowl and add each beaten egg to the batter. Continue mixing on medium thoroughly.
4. Pour the batter into an ungreased tube pan and bake for 30-40 minutes.
5. Allow the cake to cool for 20 minutes.
6. Unmold the cake and serve.

Mixer

Large bowl

Tube baking pan

Sandy P's Perfect Pudding Cake

TIP
Place the bowl and beaters in the refrigerator for 20-30 minutes before beating the cream to help whip the cream fast.

3 small boxes instant chocolate pudding
3 cups milk
1 box graham cracker cookies
1 carton heavy cream (8 ounces)
1 teaspoon confectioners sugar

1. Make 3 boxes of instant chocolate pudding following the directions on the package in a large bowl. Use 1 cup of milk per box.
2. Line a 9 x 12 pan with 1 layer of graham cracker cookies.
3. Spread the chocolate pudding and repeat layering the graham cracker and the pudding until you use all the pudding up.
4. Refrigerate for 2 hours.
5. Before serving, whip the heavy cream with a hand mixer in a bowl. While beating, add 1 teaspoon confectioners sugar. Whip the cream until stiff but don't over beat or it will turn into butter!!
6. Spread the whipped cream over top layer of graham crackers. Serve.

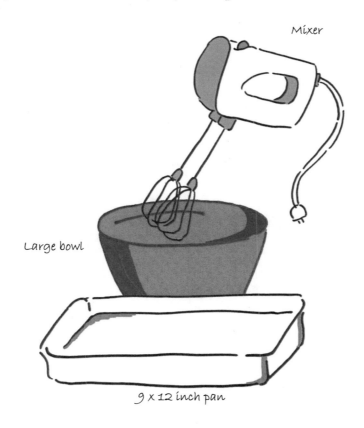

Mixer

Large bowl

9 x 12 inch pan

Tracey S's Tantalizing Trifle

1 frozen pound or sponge cake thawed
1 1/4 cup strawberry or raspberry preserves
1 large ripe banana peeled
2 containers refrigerated ready to eat pudding (4 ounces each)
1 cup frozen whipped topping thawed

1. Cut the cake into 1 inch cubes and divide it into 4 stemmed glasses or dessert bowls.
2. Heat the preserves in a microwave proof glass bowl for about 20 seconds on High to make it into a liquid.
3. Drizzle the preserves over each portion of cake.
4. Cut up the banana into thin slices.
5. Divide the banana, pudding and whipped topping evenly and add to each glass or bowl.

TIP
If you have a large glass bowl you can make a large trifle by layering the ingredients instead of dividing it into four servings.

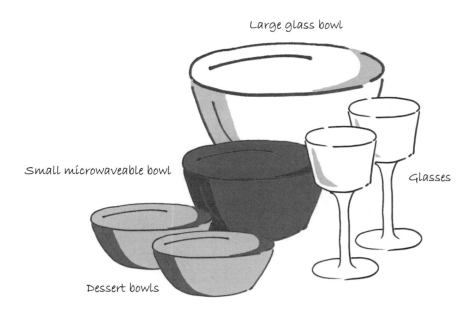

Large glass bowl

Small microwaveable bowl

Glasses

Dessert bowls

Irene K's I Scream For Ice Cream And Pound Cake

1 sliced pound cake
1/4 cup chocolate-hazelnut spread
1/4 cup chopped nut ice cream topping
1 pint any flavor favorite ice cream

1. Preheat the broiler to 500° or high.
2. Place the pound cake slices on a rimmed cookie sheet and toast them in the broiler for 1 minute on each side or until lightly browned.
3. Cool them slightly.
4. Spread one side of each slice of cake with the chocolate-hazelnut spread.
5. Place a scoop of ice cream on each slice.
6. Top with nut topping.

TIP
You can substitute angel food cake, pudding cake or any other plain cake for the pound cake in this recipe.

TIP
Whipped cream and fresh fruit make excellent toppings as well.

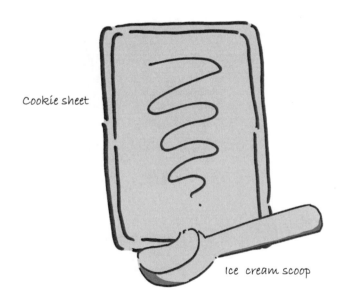

Cookie sheet

Ice cream scoop

Mary L's Loaf Banana Bread

1 package banana bread or muffin mix
3/4 cup semisweet chocolate chips
1/2 cup chopped walnuts (optional)
1/2 cup all purpose flour
2 tablespoons sugar
2 tablespoons brown sugar
1/4 cup butter or margarine
no-stick baking spray with flour (available in the baking aisle)

TIP
Putting a few pieces of apple peel in the container with brown sugar will help stop it from getting hard or lumpy. Just replace the peel if it gets dried out.

1. Spray a loaf pan with no-stick baking spray that has flour in it.
2. Prepare the banana bread batter according to directions on the box.
3. Pour the banana bread batter into the prepared loaf pan.
4. Mix the chocolate chips, nuts, flour and both sugars in a small bowl using a wooden spoon.
5. Put the margarine or butter in a medium bowl and cut it up using two knives into small pieces. Add it to the chocolate chip mixture and mix. It should resemble coarse crumbs.
6. Top the batter with the crumb mixture.
7. Bake according to package directions.

TIP
You can buy nuts already chopped or put them in a plastic bag, close it up and strike them a few times with a wooden kitchen mallet to chop them.

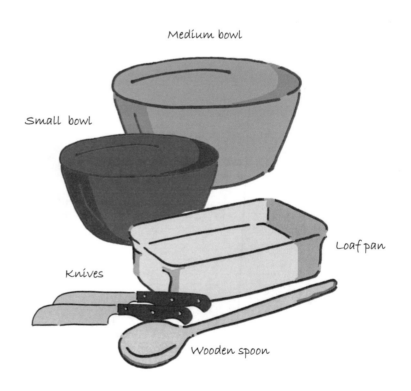

Medium bowl

Small bowl

Loaf pan

Knives

Wooden spoon

Carol L's Legendary Brookie

1 box brownie mix
2 rolls refrigerated chocolate chip cookie dough

Preheat oven to 350°

1. Prepare brownies according to package directions in a 9″ x 13″ baking pan.
2. Keep cookie dough chilled until the brownies are done.
3. Cut the cookie dough into 4 inch slices and roll the dough flat like a pancake. (Keep the brownies in the oven while you are doing this).
4. Continue making pancakes out of remaining cookie dough.
5. Remove the brownies from the oven (do not turn the oven off) and cover the brownies with the flattened cookie dough pancakes, overlapping each slightly.
6. Return to the oven and bake according to the cookie dough directions or until lightly browned.

TIP
Keep the cookie dough in the refrigerator until you are ready to roll it out in to "pancakes". This will make it easier and avoid sticking to the rolling pin.

9 x 13 baking dish

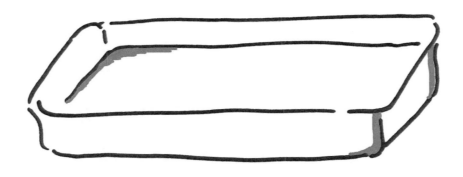

Bebe S's Brownie Cup

6 ounces semi-sweet baking chocolate
1 1/4 sticks of unsalted butter
1 cup sugar
3 eggs
3/4 cup all purpose flour
1/2 cup chopped nuts (optional)

TIP
If you cut the butter into slices, it will melt more evenly.

Preheat oven to 325°

1. Line two six cup muffin pan with paper liners.
2. Melt the chocolate and butter in a microwaveable dish at High for about 3 minutes (keep an eye on it to make sure it doesn't burn).
3. With an electric mixer beat the sugar and eggs in a large mixing bowl for about 3 minutes.
4. Lower the mixer to medium speed and add the melted chocolate and butter to the batter.
5. Gradually add the flour and mix until well blended (you can add the nuts at this time if you are using them).
6. Fill the muffin tins about 3/4 full.
7. Bake 25-30 minutes or until a toothpick comes out clean when inserted.

TIP
Baking chocolate comes in squares of 1 ounce so it makes it easy to figure out how much you need for a recipe.

TIP
You can frost these with canned frosting.

Mixer

Large bowl

Muffin tins

Muffin tin liners

Index